Michel Foucault

FEARLESS SPEECH

Edited by Joseph Pearson

Special thanks to Johanna Balusikova for design and to Sylvère
Lotringer and Ben Meyers for editing and copy-editing

© Gérard Aimé and Danielle Bancilhon for the Foucault photos on the
front cover and inside back cover, respectively.

This work received support from the French Ministry of Foreign Affairs
and the Cultural Services of the French Embassy in the United States.

Semiotext(e)
2571 W. 5th Street
Los Angeles, Ca. 90057 USA
e-mail: foreignagent@earthlink.net

CONTENTS

"My intention was not to deal with the problem of truth, but with the problem of the truth-teller, or of truth-telling as an activity: . . . who is able to tell the truth, about what, with what consequences, and with what relations to power. . . . [W]ith the question of the importance of telling the truth, knowing who is able to tell the truth, and knowing why we should tell the truth, we have the roots of what we could call the 'critical' tradition in the West."

Michel Foucault

EDITOR'S PREFACE

The following text was compiled from tape-recordings made of six lectures delivered, in English, by Michel Foucault at the University of California at Berkeley in the Fall Term of 1983. The lectures were given as part of Foucault's seminar, entitled "Discourse and Truth," devoted to the study of the Greek notion of *parrhesia* or "frankness in speaking the truth."

Since Foucault did not write, correct, or edit any part of the text which follows, it lacks his imprimatur and does not reflect his own lecture notes. What is given here constitutes only the notes of one of his auditors. Although the present text is primarily a verbatim transcription of the lectures, repetitive sentences and phrases have been eliminated, responses to questions have been incorporated, whenever possible, into the lectures themselves, more accessible translations of certain Greek texts have been substituted, and numerous sentences have been revised, all in the hope of producing a more readable set of notes. The division of the lectures into sections, the section headings, all footnotes, and a bibliography giving references to footnoted material, also have been added.

The editor gratefully acknowledges his indebtedness to John Carvalho for providing information which enabled him to audit Foucault's course. He also expresses his gratitude to Dougal Blyth for advice on various matters pertaining to the classical Greek texts Foucault discusses. In addition, he thanks Jacquelyn Taylor for her help in locating some of Foucault's references.

Joseph Pearson

Department of Philosophy, Northwestern University

1.
The Word *Parrhesia*[1]

THE MEANING OF THE WORD [2]

The word *parrhesia* [παρρησία] appears for the first time in Greek literature in Euripides [c.484–407 B.C.], and occurs throughout the ancient Greek world of letters from the end of the Fifth Century B.C. But it can also still be found in the patristic texts written at the end of the Fourth and during the Fifth Century A.D.—dozens of times, for instance, in Jean Chrysostome [A.D. 345–407].

There are three forms of the word: the nominal form *parrhesia;* the verb form *parrhesiazomai* [παρρησιάζομαι] (or better, *parrhesiazesthai* [παρρησιάζεςθαι]); and there is also the word *parrhesiastes* [παρρησιαστής], which is not very frequent and cannot be found in the Classical texts. Rather, you find it only in the Greco-Roman period—in Plutarch and Lucian, for example. In a dialogue of Lucian, "The Dead Come to Life, or The Fisherman,"[3] one of the characters also has the name Parrhesiades [Παρρησιαδής].

Parrhesia is ordinarily translated into English by "free speech" (in French by *franc-parler,* and in German by *Freimüthigkeit). Parrhesiazomai* or *parrhesiazesthai* is to use *parrhesia,* and the *parrhesiastes* is the one who uses *parrhesia,* i.e., the one who speaks the truth.

In the first part of today's seminar, I would like to give

---

1. First Lecture: 10 October 1983.
2. Cf. H. Liddell & R. Scott, "Παρρησία" in *A Greek–English Lexicon,* 1344; Pierre Miquel, "Παρρησία" in *Dictionnaire de Spiritualité,* Vol. 12, col. 260–261; and Heinrich Schlier, "Παρρησία, Παρρησιάζομαι" in *Theological Dictionary of the New Testament,* Vol. 5, 871–886.
3. Lucian, "The Dead Come to Life, or The Fisherman," Trans. A. M. Harmon in *The Works of Lucian,* Vol. 3, 1–81.

a general aperçu about the meaning of the word *parrhesia,* and
the evolution of this meaning through Greek and Roman culture.

Frankness

To begin with, what is the general meaning of the word *parrhesia?* Etymologically, *parrhesiazesthai* means "to say everything"—from *pan* [πᾶν] (everything) and *rhema* [ῥῆμα] (that
which is said). The one who uses *parrhesia,* the *parrhesiastes,* is
someone who says everything he[4] has in mind: he does not
hide anything, but opens his heart and mind completely to
other people through his discourse. In *parrhesia,* the speaker is
supposed to give a complete and exact account of what he has
in mind so that the audience is able to comprehend exactly
what the speaker thinks. The word *parrhesia,* then, refers to a
type of relationship between the speaker and what he says. For
in *parrhesia,* the speaker makes it manifestly clear and obvious
that what he says is his *own* opinion. And he does this by
avoiding any kind of rhetorical form which would veil what he
thinks. Instead, the *parrhesiastes* uses the most direct words
and forms of expression he can find. Whereas rhetoric provides the speaker with technical devices to help him prevail
upon the minds of his audience (*regardless* of the rhetorician's
own opinion concerning what he says), in *parrhesia,* the *parrhesiastes* acts on other people's minds by showing them as
directly as possible what he actually believes.

If we distinguish between the speaking subject (the subject
of enunciation) and the grammatical subject of the enounced,

---

4. Responding to a student's question, Foucault indicated that the
oppressed role of women in Greek society generally deprived them of the
use of *parrhesia* (along with aliens, slaves, and children). Hence the predominant use of the masculine pronoun throughout.

we could say that there is also the subject of the enunciandum— which refers to the held belief or opinion of the speaker. In *parrhesia* the speaker emphasizes the fact that he is both the subject of the enunciation and the subject of the enunciandum—that he himself is the subject of the opinion to which he refers. The specific "speech activity" of the parrhesiastic enunciation thus takes the form: "I am the one who thinks this and that." I use the phrase "speech activity" rather than John Searle's "speech act" (or Austin's "performative utterance") in order to distinguish the parrhesiastic utterance and its commitments from the usual sorts of commitment which obtain between someone and what he or she says. For, as we shall see, the commitment involved in *parrhesia* is linked to a certain social situation, to a difference of status between the speaker and his audience, to the fact that the *parrhesiastes* says something which is dangerous to himself and thus involves a risk, and so on.

Truth

There are two types of *parrhesia* which we must distinguish. First, there is a pejorative sense of the word not very far from "chattering," and which consists in saying any- or everything one has in mind without qualification. This pejorative sense occurs in Plato,[5] for example, as a characterization of the bad democratic constitution where everyone has the right to address his fellow citizens and to tell them anything—even the most stupid or dangerous things for the city. This pejorative meaning is also found more frequently in Christian literature where such "bad" *parrhesia* is opposed to silence as a

---

5. Plato, *Republic* 577b. Cf. also *Phaedrus* 240e & *Laws* 649b, 671b.

discipline or as the requisite condition for the contemplation of God.[6] As a verbal activity which reflects every movement of the heart and mind, *parrhesia* in this negative sense is obviously an obstacle to the contemplation of God.

Most of the time, however, *parrhesia* does not have this pejorative meaning in the classical texts, but rather a positive one. *Parrhesiazesthai* means "to tell the truth." But does the *parrhesiastes* say what he *thinks* is true, or does he say what *is* really true? To my mind, the *parrhesiastes* says what is true because he *knows* that it *is* true; and he *knows* that it is true because it is really true. The *parrhesiastes* is not only sincere and says what is his opinion, but his opinion is also the truth. He says what he *knows* to be true. The second characteristic of *parrhesia*, then, is that there is always an exact coincidence between belief and truth.

It would be interesting to compare Greek *parrhesia* with the modern (Cartesian) conception of evidence. For since Descartes, the coincidence between belief and truth is obtained in a certain (mental) evidential experience. For the Greeks, however, the coincidence between belief and truth does not take place in a (mental) experience, but in a *verbal activity*, namely, *parrhesia*. It appears that *parrhesia*, in this Greek sense, can no longer occur in our modern epistemological framework.

I should note that I never found any texts in ancient Greek culture where the *parrhesiastes* seems to have any *doubts* about his own possession of the truth. And indeed, that is the difference between the Cartesian problem and the parrhesias-

---

6. Cf. G. J. M. Bartelink, "Quelques observations sur παρρησία dans la littérature paléo-chrétienne," in *Graecitas et latinitas Christianorum primaeva*, Supplement III, 44–55 [παρρησία au sens péjoratif].

tic attitude. For before Descartes obtains indubitably clear and distinct evidence, he is not certain that what he believes is, in fact, true. In the Greek conception of *parrhesia*, however, there does not seem to be a problem about the acquisition of the truth since such truth-having is guaranteed by the possession of certain *moral* qualities: when someone has certain moral qualities, then that is the proof that he has access to truth—and vice versa. The "parrhesiastic game" presupposes that the *parrhesiastes* is someone who has the moral qualities which are required, first, to know the truth, and, secondly, to convey such truth to others.[7]

If there is a kind of "proof" of the sincerity of the *parrhesiastes*, it is his *courage*. The fact that a speaker says something dangerous—different from what the majority believes—is a strong indication that he is a *parrhesiastes*. If we raise the question of how we can know whether someone is a truth-teller, we raise two questions. First, how is it that we can know whether some particular individual is a truth-teller; and secondly, how is it that the alleged *parrhesiastes* can be certain that what he believes is, in fact, the truth. The first question—recognizing someone as a *parrhesiastes*—was a very important one in Greco-Roman society, and, as we shall see, was explicitly raised and discussed by Plutarch, Galen, and others. The second sceptical question, however, is a particularly modern one which, I believe, is foreign to the Greeks.

Danger

Someone is said to use *parrhesia* and merits consideration as a

---

7. Cf. Foucault interview, "On the Genealogy of Ethics: An Overview of Work in Progress," in H. L. Dreyfus & P. Rabinow, *Michel Foucault*, 252.

parrhesiastes only if there is a risk or danger for him in telling the truth. For instance, from the ancient Greek perspective, a grammar teacher may tell the truth to the children that he teaches, and indeed may have no doubt that what he teaches is true. But in spite of this coincidence between belief and truth, he is not a *parrhesiastes*. However, when a philosopher address-es himself to a sovereign, to a tyrant, and tells him that his tyranny is disturbing and unpleasant because tyranny is incompatible with justice, then the philosopher speaks the truth, believes he is speaking the truth, and, more than that, also takes a *risk* (since the tyrant may become angry, may pun-ish him, may exile him, may kill him). And that was exactly Plato's situation with Dionysius in Syracuse—concerning which there are very interesting references in Plato's Seventh Letter, and also in *The Life of Dion* by Plutarch. I hope we shall study these texts later.

So you see, the *parrhesiastes* is someone who takes a risk. Of course, this risk is not always a risk of life. When, for example, you see a friend doing something wrong and you risk incurring his anger by telling him he is wrong, you are acting as a *parrhe-siastes*. In such a case, you do not risk your life, but you may hurt him by your remarks, and your friendship may consequently suffer for it. If, in a political debate, an orator risks losing his popularity because his opinions are contrary to the majority's opinion, or his opinions may usher in a political scandal, he uses *parrhesia*. *Parrhesia*, then, is linked to courage in the face of danger: it demands the courage to speak the truth in spite of some danger. And in its extreme form, telling the truth takes place in the "game" of life or death.

It is because the *parrhesiastes* must take a risk in speaking the truth that the king or tyrant generally cannot use *parrhesia;* for *he* risks nothing.

When you accept the parrhesiastic game in which your own life is exposed, you are taking up a specific relationship to yourself: you risk death to tell the truth instead of reposing in the security of a life where the truth goes unspoken. Of course, the threat of death comes from the Other, and thereby requires a relationship to the Other. But the *parrhesiastes* primarily chooses a specific relationship to himself: he prefers himself as a truth-teller rather than as a living being who is false to himself.

Criticism

If, during a trial, you say something which can be used against you, you may not be using *parrhesia* in spite of the fact that you are sincere, that you believe what you say is true, and you are endangering yourself in so speaking. For in *parrhesia* the danger always comes from the fact that the said truth is capable of hurting or angering the *interlocutor*. *Parrhesia* is thus always a "game" between the one who speaks the truth and the interlocutor. The *parrhesia* involved, for example, may be the advice that the interlocutor should behave in a certain way, or that he is wrong in what he thinks, or in the way he acts, and so on. Or the *parrhesia* may be a confession of what the speaker himself has done insofar as he makes this confession to someone who exercises power over him, and is able to censure or punish him for what he has done. So you see, the function of *parrhesia* is not to demonstrate the truth to someone else, but has the function of *criticism:* criticism of the interlocutor or of the speaker himself. "This is what you do and this is what you think; but that is what you should not do or should not think." "This is the way you behave, but that is the way you ought to behave." "This is what I have done, and was wrong in so doing." *Parrhesia* is a form of criticism, either towards another or towards oneself, but always in a situation where the

speaker or confessor is in a position of inferiority with respect
to the interlocutor. The *parrhesiastes* is always less powerful
than the one with whom he speaks. The *parrhesia* comes from
"below," as it were, and is directed towards "above." This is
why an ancient Greek would not say that a teacher or father
who criticizes a child uses *parrhesia*. But when a philosopher
criticizes a tyrant, when a citizen criticizes the majority, when
a pupil criticizes his teacher, then such speakers may be using
parrhesia.

This is not to imply, however, that *anyone* can use *parrhesia*. For although there is a text in Euripides where a servant
uses *parrhesia*,[8] most of the time the use of *parrhesia* requires
that the *parrhesiastes* know his own genealogy, his own status;
i.e., usually one must first be a male citizen to speak the truth
as a *parrhesiastes*. Indeed, someone who is deprived of *parrhesia*
is in the same situation as a slave to the extent that he cannot
take part in the political life of the city, nor play the "parrhesiastic game." In "democratic parrhesia"—where one speaks to
the assembly, the *ekklesia*—one must be a citizen; in fact, one
must be one of the *best* among the citizens, possessing those
specific personal, moral, and social qualities which grant one
the privilege to speak.

However, the *parrhesiastes* risks his privilege to speak freely
when he discloses a truth which threatens the majority. For it
was a well-known juridical situation that Athenian leaders were
exiled only because they proposed something which was
opposed by the majority, or even because the assembly thought
that the strong influence of certain leaders limited its own freedom. And so the assembly was, in this manner, "protected"

---

8. Euripides, *The Bacchae*, 666ff.

against the truth. That, then, is the institutional background of "democratic *parrhesia*"—which must be distinguished from that "monarchic *parrhesia*" where an advisor gives the sovereign honest and helpful advice.

Duty

The last characteristic of *parrhesia* is this: in *parrhesia,* telling the truth is regarded as a *duty*. The orator who speaks the truth to those who cannot accept his truth, for instance, and who may be exiled, or punished in some way, is *free* to keep silent. No one forces him to speak, but he feels that it is his duty to do so. When, on the other hand, someone is compelled to tell the truth (as, for example, under duress of torture), then his discourse is not a parrhesiastic utterance. A criminal who is forced by his judges to confess his crime does not use *parrhesia*. But if he voluntarily confesses his crime to someone else out of a sense of moral obligation, then he performs a parrhesiastic act. To criticize a friend or a sovereign is an act of *parrhesia* insofar as it is a duty to help a friend who does not recognize his wrongdoing, or insofar as it is a duty towards the city to help the king to better himself as a sovereign. *Parrhesia* is thus related to freedom and to duty.

To summarize the foregoing, *parrhesia* is a kind of verbal activity where the speaker has a specific relation to truth through frankness, a certain relationship to his own life through danger, a certain type of relation to himself or other people through criticism (self-criticism or criticism of other people), and a specific relation to moral law through freedom and duty. More precisely, *parrhesia* is a verbal activity in which a speaker expresses his personal relationship to truth, and risks his life because he recognizes truth-telling as a duty to improve or help other people (as well as himself). In *parrhesia,* the speaker uses his freedom and chooses frankness instead of persuasion, truth instead of falsehood or silence, the risk of death instead of life and security, criticism instead of flattery, and moral duty instead of self-interest and moral apathy. That then, quite generally, is the positive meaning of the word *parrhesia* in most of the Greek texts where it occurs from the Fifth Century B.C. to the Fifth Century A.D.

EVOLUTION OF THE WORD

Now what I would like to do in this seminar is not to study and analyze all the dimensions and features of *parrhesia*, but rather to show and to emphasize some aspects of the evolution of the parrhesiastic game in ancient culture (from the Fifth Century B.C.) to the beginnings of Christianity. And I think that we can analyze this evolution from three points of view.

Rhetoric

The first concerns the relationship of *parrhesia* to rhetoric— a relationship which is problematic even in Euripides. In the Socratic-Platonic tradition, *parrhesia* and rhetoric stand in strong opposition; and this opposition appears very clearly in the *Gorgias*, for example, where the word *parrhesia* occurs.[9] The continuous long speech is a rhetorical or sophistical device, whereas the dialogue through questions and answers is typical for *parrhesia*; i.e., dialogue is a major technique for playing the parrhesiastic game.

The opposition of *parrhesia* and rhetoric also runs through

---

9. Plato, *Gorgias* 461e, 487a–e, 491e

the *Phaedrus*—where, as you know, the main problem is not about the nature of the opposition between speech and writing, but concerns the difference between the *logos* which speaks the truth and the *logos* which is not capable of such truth-telling. This opposition between *parrhesia* and rhetoric, which is so clear-cut in the Fourth Century B.C. throughout Plato's writings, will last for centuries in the philosophical tradition. In Seneca, for example, one finds the idea that personal conversations are the best vehicle for frank speaking and truth-telling insofar as one can dispense, in such conversations, with the need for rhetorical devices and ornamentation. And even during the Second Century A.D. the cultural opposition between rhetoric and philosophy is still very clear and important.

However, one can also find some signs of the incorporation of *parrhesia* within the field of rhetoric in the work of rhetoricians at the beginning of the Empire. In Quintillian's *Institutio Oratoria*[10] for example (Book IX, Chapter II), Quintillian explains that some rhetorical figures are specifically adapted for intensifying the emotions of the audience; and such technical figures he calls by the name *exclamatio* (exclamation). Related to these exclamations is a kind of natural exclamation which, Quintillian notes, is not "simulated or artfully designed." This type of natural exclamation he calls "free speech" [*libera oratione*] which, he tells us, was called "license" [*licentia*] by Cornificius, and "*parrhesia*" by the Greeks. *Parrhesia* is thus a sort of "figure" among rhetorical figures, but with this characteristic: that it is without any figure since it is completely natural. *Parrhesia* is the zero degree of those rhetorical figures which intensify the emotions of the audience.

---

10. Quintillian, *The Institutio Oratoria of Quintillian*, Vol. 3, 389–439.

Politics

The second important aspect of the evolution of *parrhesia* is related to the political field.[11] As it appears in Euripides' plays and also in the texts of the Fourth Century B.C., *parrhesia* is an essential characteristic of Athenian democracy. Of course, we still have to investigate the role of *parrhesia* in the Athenian constitution. But we can say quite generally that *parrhesia* was a guideline for democracy as well as an ethical and personal attitude characteristic of the good citizen. Athenian democracy was defined very explicitly as a constitution (*politeia*) in which people enjoyed *demokratia, isegoria* (the equal right of speech), *isonomia* (the equal participation of all citizens in the exercise of power), and *parrhesia*. *Parrhesia*, which is a requisite for public speech, takes place between citizens as individuals, and also between citizens construed as an assembly. Moreover, the *agora* is the place where *parrhesia* appears.

During the Hellenistic period this political meaning changes with the rise of the Hellenic monarchies. *Parrhesia* now becomes centered in the relationship between the sovereign and his advisors or court men. In the monarchic constitution of the state, it is the advisor's duty to use *parrhesia* to help the king with his decisions, and to prevent him from abusing his power. *Parrhesia* is necessary and useful both for the king and for the people under his rule. The sovereign himself is not a *parrhesiastes*, but a touchstone of the good

11. *Cf.* Pierre Miquel, "Παρρησία" in *Dictionnaire de Spiritualité*, Vol. 12, col. 260–261; Erik Peterson, "Zur Bedeutungsgeschichte von "Παρρησία" in *Reinhold Seeberg Festschrift*, Bd. 1, 283–288; Giuseppe Scarpat, *Parrhesia. Storia del termine e delle sue traduzioni in Latino*, 29ff; Heinrich Schlier, "Παρρησία, παρρησιάζομαι" in *Theological Dictionary of the New Testament* Vol. 5, 871–873.

ruler is his ability to play the parrhesiastic game. Thus, a good king accepts everything that a genuine *parrhesiastes* tells him, even if it turns out to be unpleasant for him to hear criticisms of his decisions. A sovereign shows himself to be a tyrant if he disregards his honest advisors, or punishes them for what they have said. The portrayal of a sovereign by most Greek historians takes into account the way he behaves towards his advisors—as if such behavior were an index of his ability to hear the *parrhesiastes*.

There is also a third category of players in the monarchic parrhesiastic game, viz., the silent majority: the people in general who are not present at the exchanges between the king and his advisors, but to whom, and on behalf of whom, the advisors refer when offering advice to the king.

The place where *parrhesia* appears in the context of monarchic rule is the king's court, and no longer the *agora*.

Philosophy

Finally, *parrhesia's* evolution can be traced through its relation to the field of philosophy—regarded as an art of life *(techne tou biou)*.

In the writings of Plato, Socrates appears in the role of the *parrhesiastes*. Although the word *parrhesia* appears several times in Plato, he never uses the word *parrhesiastes*—a word which only appears later as part of the Greek vocabulary. And yet the role of Socrates is typically a parrhesiastic one, for he constantly confronts Athenians in the street and, as noted in the *Apology*,[12] points out the truth to them, bidding them to care for wisdom, truth, and the perfection of their souls. And in the

---

12. Plato, *Apology* 29d–e.

Alcibiades Major, as well, Socrates assumes a parrhesiastic role in the dialogue. For whereas Alcibiades' friends and lovers all flatter him in their attempt to obtain his favors, Socrates risks provoking Alcibiades' anger when he leads him to this idea: that before Alcibiades will be able to accomplish what he is so set on achieving, viz., to became the first among the Athenians to rule Athens and become more powerful than the King of Persia, before he will be able to take care of Athens, he must first learn to take care of himself. Philosophical *parrhesia* is thus associated with the theme of the care of oneself *(epimeleia heautou)*.[13]

By the time of the Epicureans, *parrhesia's* affinity with the care of oneself developed to the point where *parrhesia* itself was primarily regarded as a *techne* of spiritual guidance for the "education of the soul." Philodemus [c. 110–35 B.C.], for example (who, with Lucretius [c. 99–55 B.C.], was one of the most significant Epicurean writers during the First Century B.C.), wrote a book about *parrhesia* [Περὶ παρρηδίας][14] which concerns technical practices useful for teaching and helping one another in the Epicurean community. We shall examine some of these parrhesiastic techniques as they developed in, for example, the Stoic philosophies of Epictetus, Seneca, and others.

---

13. Cf. Michel Foucault, *Le Souci de soi*, 58ff.
14. Philodemus, Περὶ παρρηδίας, Ed. A. Olivieri. Leipzig, 1914.

2.
Parrhesia in Euripides [15]

Today I would like to begin analyzing the first occurrences of the word *parrhesia* in Greek literature. Specifically, I want to examine the use of the word in six tragedies of Euripides: *Phoenician Women; Hippolytus; The Bacchae; Electra; Ion;* and *Orestes.*

In the first four plays, *parrhesia* does not constitute an important topic or *motif;* but the word itself generally occurs within a precise context which aids our understanding of its meaning. In the last two plays—*Ion* and *Orestes*—*parrhesia* does assume a very important role. Indeed, I think that *Ion* is entirely devoted to the problem of *parrhesia* since it pursues the question: who has the right, the duty, and the courage to speak the truth? This parrhesiastic problem in *Ion* is raised in the framework of the relations between the gods and human beings. In *Orestes*—which was written ten years later, and therefore is one of Euripides' last plays—the role of *parrhesia* is not nearly as significant. And yet the play still contains a parrhesiastic scene which warrants attention insofar as it is directly related to political issues that the Athenians were then raising. Here, in this parrhesiastic scene, there is a transition regarding the question of *parrhesia* as it occurs in the context of human institutions. Specifically, *parrhesia* is seen as both a political and a philosophical issue.

Today, then, I shall first try to say something about the occurrences of the word *parrhesia* in the first four plays mentioned in order to throw some more light on the meaning of the word. And then I shall attempt a global analysis of *Ion* as the decisive parrhesiastic play where we see human beings taking upon themselves the role of truth-tellers—a role which the gods are no longer able to assume.

---

15. Second Lecture: 31 October 1983.

THE PHOENICIAN WOMEN [C.411–409 B.C.]

Consider, first, *The Phoenician Women*. The major theme of this play concerns the fight between Oedipus' two sons: Eteocles and Polyneices.

Recall that after Oedipus' fall, in order to avoid their father's curse that they should divide his inheritance "by sharpened steel," Eteocles and Polyneices make a pact to rule over Thebes alternately, year by year, with Eteocles (who was older) reigning first. But after his initial year of reign, Eteocles refuses to hand over the crown and yield power to his brother, Polyneices. Eteocles thus represents tyranny, and Polyneices—who lives in exile—represents the democratic regime. Seeking his share of his father's crown, Polyneices returns with an army of Argives in order to overthrow Eteocles and lay siege to the city of Thebes. It is in the hope of avoiding this confrontation that Jocasta—the mother of Polyneices and Eteocles, and the wife and mother of Oedipus— persuades her two sons to meet in a truce. When Polyneices arrives for this meeting, Jocasta asks Polyneices about his suf- fering during the time he was exiled from Thebes. "Is it real- ly hard to be exiled?" asks Jocasta. And Polyneices answers, "Worse than anything." And when Jocasta asks why exile is so hard, Polyneices replies that it is because one cannot enjoy *parrhesia:*

> JOCASTA: This above all I long to know: What is an exile's life? Is it great misery?
> POLYNEICES: The greatest; worse in reality than in report.
> JOCASTA: Worse in what way? What chiefly galls an exile's heart?

POLYNEICES: The worst is this: right of free speech
does not exist. [ἓν μὲν μέγιστον, οὐκ ἔχει παρρησίαν.]
JOCASTA: That's a slave's life—to be forbidden to
speak one's mind.
POLYNEICES: One has to endure the idiocy of those
who rule.
JOCASTA: To join fools in their foolishness—that
makes one sick.
POLYNEICES: One finds it pays to deny nature and be
a slave.[16]

As you can see from these few lines, *parrhesia* is linked,
first of all, to Polyneices' social status. For if you are not a regular citizen in the city, if you are exiled, then you cannot use
parrhesia. That is quite obvious. But something else is also
implied, viz., that if you do not have the right of free speech,
you are unable to exercise any kind of power, and thus you are
in the same situation as a slave. Further: if such citizens cannot use *parrhesia*, they cannot oppose a ruler's power. And
without the right of criticism, the power exercised by a sovereign is without limitation. Such power without limitation is
characterized by Jocasta as "joining fools in their foolishness."
For power without limitation is directly related to madness.
The man who exercises power is wise only insofar as there
exists someone who can use *parrhesia* to criticize him, thereby
putting some limit to his power, to his command.

---

16. Euripides, *The Phoenician Women*. Trans. Philip Vellacott, lines 386–394.

HIPPOLYTUS [428 B.C.]

The second passage from Euripides I want to quote comes from *Hippolytus.* As you know, the play is about Phaedra's love for Hippolytus. And the passage concerning *parrhesia* occurs just after Phaedra's confession: when Phaedra, early on in the play, confesses her love for Hippolytus to her nurse (without, however, actually saying his name). But the word *parrhesia* does not concern this confession, but refers to something quite different. For just after her confession of her love for Hippolytus, Phaedra speaks of those noble and high-born women from royal households who first brought shame upon their own family, upon their husband and children, by committing adultery with other men. And Phaedra says she does not want to do the same since she wants her sons to live in Athens, proud of their mother, and exercising *parrhesia.* And she claims that if a man is conscious of a stain in his family, he becomes a slave:

> PHAEDRA: I will never be known to bring dishonour on my husband or my children. I want my two sons to go back and live in glorious Athens, hold their heads high there, and speak their minds there like free men [ἐλεύθεροι ταρρησία θάλλοντες], honored for their mother's name. One thing can make the most bold-spirited man a slave: to know the secret of a parent's shameful act.[17]

In this text we see, once again, a connection between the lack of *parrhesia* and slavery. For if you cannot speak freely

---

17. Euripides, *Hippolytus.* Trans. Philip Vellacott, lines 420–425.

because you are aware of dishonor in your family, then you are enslaved. Also, citizenship by itself does not appear to be sufficient to obtain and guarantee the exercise of free speech. Honor, a good reputation for oneself and one's family, is also needed before one can freely address the people of the city. *Parrhesia* thus requires both moral and social qualifications which come from a noble birth and a respectful reputation.

THE BACCHAE [C.407–406 B.C.]

In *The Bacchae* there is a very short passage, a transitional moment, where the word appears. One of Pentheus' servants—a herdsman [βοσκός] and messenger [ἀγγελος] to the king—has come to report about the confusion and disorder the Maenads are generating in the community, and the fantastic deeds they are committing. But, as you know, it is an old tradition that messengers who bring glad tidings are rewarded for the news they convey, whereas those who bring bad news are exposed to punishment. And so the king's servant is very reluctant to deliver his ill tidings to Pentheus. But he asks the king whether he may use *parrhesia* and tell him everything he knows, for he fears the king's wrath. And Pentheus promises that he will not get into trouble so long as he speaks the truth:

HERDSMAN: I have seen the holy Bacchae, who like a flight of spears went streaming bare-limbed, frantic, out of the city gate. I have come with the intention of telling you, my lord, and the city, of their strange and terrible doings—things beyond all wonder. But first I would learn whether I may speak freely [παρρηδια φραδω] of what is going on there, or if I should trim my words. I fear your hastiness, my lord, your anger, your too potent royalty.

PENTHEUS: From me fear nothing. Say all that you
have to say; anger should not grow hot against the innocent. The more dreadful your story of these Bacchic rites,
the heavier punishment I will inflict upon this man who
enticed our women to their evil ways.[18]

These lines are interesting because they show a case
where the *parrhesiastes*, the one who speaks the truth, is not an
entirely free man, but a servant to the king—one who cannot
use *parrhesia* if the king is not wise enough to enter into the
parrhesiastic game and grant him permission to speak openly.
For if the king lacks self-mastery, if he is carried away by his
passions and gets mad at the messenger, then he does not hear
the truth, and will also be a bad ruler for the city. But
Pentheus, as a wise king, offers his servant what we can call
a "parrhesiastic contract."

The "parrhesiastic contract"—which became relatively
important in the political life of rulers in the Greco-Roman
world—consists in the following. The sovereign, the one who
has power but lacks the truth, addresses himself to the one
who has the truth but lacks power, and tells him: if you tell me
the truth, no matter what this truth turns out to be, you won't
be punished; and those who are responsible for any injustices
will be punished, but not those who speak the truth about
such injustices. This idea of the "parrhesiastic contract"
became associated with *parrhesia* as a special privilege granted
to the best and most honest citizens of the city. Of course, the
parrhesiastic contract between Pentheus and his messenger is

---

18. Euripides, *The Bacchae*. Trans. Philip Vellacott, lines 664–676.

only a moral obligation since it lacks all institutional founda-
tion. As the king's servant, the messenger is still quite vulnerable, and still takes a risk in speaking. But, although he is
courageous, he is also not reckless, and is cautious about the
consequences of what he might say. The "contract" is intended to limit the risk he takes in speaking.

ELECTRA [415 B.C.]

In *Electra* the word *parrhesia* occurs in the confrontation
between Electra and her mother, Clytemnestra. I do not need
to remind you of this famous story, but only to indicate that
prior to the moment in the play when the word appears,
Orestes has just killed the tyrant Aegisthus—Clytemnestra's
lover and co-murderer (with Clytemnestra) of Agamemnon
(Clytemnestra's husband and father to Orestes and Electra).
But right before Clytemnestra appears on the scene, Orestes
hides himself and Aegisthus' body. So when Clytemnnestra
makes her entry, she is not aware of what has just transpired,
i.e., she does not know that Aegisthus has just been killed.
And her entry is very beautiful and solemn, for she is riding in
a royal chariot surrounded by the most beautiful of the captive
maidens of Troy, all of whom are now her slaves. And Electra,
who is there when her mother arrives, also behaves like a slave
in order to hide the fact that the moment of revenge for her
father's death is at hand. She is also there to insult
Clytemnestra, and to remind her of her crime. This dramatic
scene gives way to a confrontation between the two. A discussion begins, and we have two parallel speeches, both equally
long (forty lines), the first one by Clytemnestra, and the second
by Electra.

Clytemnestra's speech begins with the words "λέξω δέ" "I will speak" [l. 1013]. And she proceeds to tell the truth, confessing that she killed Agamemnon as a punishment for the sacrificial death of her daughter, Iphigeneia. Following this speech, Electra replies, beginning with the symmetrical formulation "λέγοιμ᾽ ἄν"—"then, I will speak" [l. 1060]. In spite of this symmetry, however, there is a very clear difference between the two. For at the end of her speech, Clytemnestra addresses Electra directly and says to her, "Use your *parrhesia* to prove that I was wrong to kill your father":

> CLYTEMNESTRA: ...I killed him. I took the only way open to me—turned for help to his enemies. Well, what could I do? None of your father's friends would have helped me murder him. So if you're anxious to refute me, do it now; speak freely [κἀντίθες παρρησίᾳ]; prove your father's death not justified.[19]

And, after the Chorus speaks, Electra replies, "Do not forget your latest words, mother. You gave me parrhesia towards you":

> ELECTRA: Mother, remember what you said just now. You promised that I might state my opinion freely without fear [διδοῦσα πρὸς σέ μοι παρρησίαν].[20]

And Clytemnestra answers: "I said so, daughter, and I meant it" [1.1057]. But Electra is still wary and cautious, for she wonders whether her mother will listen to her only to hurt her afterwards:

---

19. Euripides, *Electra*. Trans. Philip Vellacott, lines 1046–1050.
20. *Ibid.*, 1055-1056.

ELECTRA: Do you mean you'll listen first, and get your own back afterwards?

CLYTEMNESTRA: No, no; you're free to say what your heart wants to say.

ELECTRA: I'll say it, then. This is where I'll begin...[21]

And Electra proceeds to speak openly, blaming her mother for what she has done.

There is another asymmetrical aspect between these two discourses which concerns the difference in status of the two speakers. For Clytemnestra is the queen, and does not use or require *parrhesia* to plead for her own defense in killing Agamemnon. But Electra—who is in the situation of a slave, who plays the role of a slave in this scene, who can no longer live in her father's house under her father's protection, and who addresses her mother just as a servant would address the queen—Electra needs the right of *parrhesia*.

And so another parrhesiastic contract is drawn between Clytemnestra and Electra: Clytemnestra promises she will not punish Electra for her frankness just as Pentheus promised his messenger in *The Bacchae*. But in *Electra*, the parrhesiastic contract is subverted. It is not subverted by Clytemnestra (who, as the queen, still has the power to punish Electra); it is subverted by Electra herself. Electra asks her mother to promise her that she will not be punished for speaking frankly, and Clytemnestra makes such a promise without knowing that she, Clytemnestra herself, will be punished for her confession. For, a few minutes later, she is subsequently killed by her children, Orestes and Electra. Thus the parrhesiastic contract is subverted: the one who was granted the privilege of *parrhesia*

---

21. *Ibid.*, lines 1058–1060.

is not harmed, but the one who granted the right of *parrhesia* is—and by the very person who, in the inferior position, was asking for *parrhesia*. The parrhesiastic contract becomes a subversive trap for Clytemnestra.

ION [c.418–417 B.C.]

We turn now to *Ion,* a parrhesiastic play.

The mythological framework of the play involves the legendary founding of Athens. According to Attic myth, Erectheus was the first king of Athens—born a son of Earth and returning to Earth in death. Erectheus thus personifies that of which the Athenians were so proud, viz., their autochthony: that they literally were sprung from Athenian soil.[22] In 418 B.C., about the time when this play was written, such mythological reference had political meaning. For Euripides wanted to remind his audience that the Athenians are native to Athenian soil; but through the character of Xuthus (husband to Erectheus' daughter Creusa, and a foreigner to Athens since he comes from Phthia), Euripides also wanted to indicate to his audience that the Athenians are related, through this marriage, to the people of the Peloponese, and specifically to Achaia—named from one of the sons of Xuthus and Creusa: Achaeus. For Euripides' account of the pan-Hellenic nature of Athenian genealogy makes Ion the son of Apollo and Creusa (daughter to Athens' ancient king Erectheus). Creusa later marries Xuthus (who was an ally of the Athenians in their war against the Euboeans [ll. 58–62]).

---

22. Cf. Plato, *Menexenus* 237b.

Two sons are born from this marriage: Dorus and Achaeus [l. 1590]. Ion was said to be the founder of the Ionic people; Dorus, the founder of the Dorians; and Achaeus, the founder of the Achaeans. Thus all of the ancestors of the Greek race are depicted as descended from the royal house of Athens.[23]

Euripides' reference to Creusa's relationship with Apollo, as well as his placement of the play's setting at the Temple of Apollo at Delphi, is meant to exhibit the close relationship between Athens and Phoebus Apollo—the pan-Hellenic god of the Delphic sanctuary. For at the historical moment of the play's production in ancient Greece, Athens was trying to forge a pan-Hellenic coalition against Sparta. Rivalry existed between Athens and Delphi since the Delphic priests were primarily on the side of the Spartans. But, to put Athens in the favorable position of leader of the Hellenic world, Euripides wished to emphasize the relations of mutual parenthood between the two cities. These mythological genealogies, then, are meant, in part, to justify Athens' imperialistic politics towards other Greek cities at a time when Athenian leaders still thought an Athenian Empire was possible.

I shall not focus on the political and mythological aspects of the play, but on the theme of the shift of the place of truth's disclosure from Delphi to Athens. As you know, the oracle at Delphi was supposed to be the place in Greece where human beings were told the truth by the gods through the utterances of the Pythia. But in this play, we see a very explicit shift from

---

23. On the political meaning of *Ion*, A. S. Owen writes: "Its object is to give reasons for the Athenian Empire to hold together and to make the Dorian states of the Peloponese feel that the distant past might justify them in alliance with Athens" ["Introduction" to Euripides, *Ion*. Oxford: Clarendon Press, 1957; xxii].

the oracular truth at Delphi to Athens: Athens becomes the place where truth now appears. And, as a part of this shift, truth is no longer disclosed by the gods *to* human beings (as at Delphi), but is disclosed to human beings *by* human beings through Athenian *parrhesia*.

Euripides' *Ion* is a play praising Athenian autochtony, and affirming Athens' blood-affinity with most other Greek states; but it is primarily a story of the movement of truth-telling from Delphi to Athens, from Phoebus Apollo to the Athenian citizen. And that is the reason why I think the play is the story of *parrhesia*: the decisive Greek parrhesiastic play.

Now I would like to give the following schematic aperçu of the play:

SILENCE	TRUTH	DECEPTION
Delphi	Athens (Athene)	Foreign Countries
Apollo	Erectheus	Xuthus
	Creusa	

Ion

We shall see that Apollo keeps silent throughout the drama; that Xuthus is deceived by the god, but is also a deceiver. And we shall also see how Creusa and Ion both speak the truth against Apollo's silence, for only they are connected to the Athenian earth which endows them with *parrhesia*.

Hermes' Prologue

I would first like to briefly recount the events, given in Hermes' prologue, which have taken place before the play begins.

After the death of Erectheus' other children (Cecrops, Orithyia, and Procris), Creusa is the only surviving offspring of the Athenian dynasty. One day, as a young girl, while pick-

ing yellow flowers by the Long Rocks, Apollo rapes or seduces
her [γάμοις, 1.10].

Is it a rape or a seduction? For the Greeks, the difference
is not as crucial as it is for us. Clearly, when someone rapes
a woman, a girl, or a boy, he uses physical violence; whereas
when someone seduces another, he uses words, his ability to
speak, his superior status, and so on. For the Greeks, using
one's psychological, social, or intellectual abilities to seduce
another person is not so different from using physical violence. Indeed, from the perspective of the law, seduction was
considered more criminal than rape. For when someone is
raped, it is against his or her will; but when someone is
seduced, then that constitutes the proof that at a specific
moment, the seduced individual chose to be unfaithful to his
or her wife or husband, or parents, or family. Seduction was
considered more of an attack against a spouse's power, or a family's power, since the one who was seduced chose to act against
the wishes of his or her spouse, parents, or family.[24]

In any case, Creusa is raped or seduced by Apollo, and
she becames pregnant. And when she is about to give birth, she
returns to the place where she was led by Apollo, viz., a cave
beneath Athens' acropolis—beneath the Mount of Pallas
under the center of the Athenian city. And here she hides herself until, all alone, she gives birth to a son [l. 949]. But
because she does not want her father, Erectheus, to find out
about the child (for she was ashamed of what happened), she

---

24. K. J. Dover writes: "To seduce a woman of citizen status was more
culpable than to rape her, not only because rape was presumed to be
unpremeditated but because seduction involved the capture of her affec-
tion and loyalty; it was the degree of offense against the man to whom she
belonged, not her own feelings, which mattered" ["Classical Greek
Attitudes to Sexual Behavior," 62].

exposes it, leaving the child to wild beasts. Apollo then sends his brother, Hermes, to bring the child, his cradle and clothes, to the temple at Delphi. And the boy is raised as a servant of the god in the sanctuary; and he is regarded as a foundling. For no one in Delphi (except Apollo himself) knows who he is or where he comes from; and Ion himself does not know. Ion thus appears, on the schema I outlined, between Delphi and Athens, Apollo and Creusa. For he is the son of Apollo and Creusa, and was born in Athens but lives his life in Delphi.

In Athens, Creusa does not know whatever became of her child; and she wonders whether it is dead or alive. Later she marries Xuthus, a foreigner whose alien presence immensely complicates the continuity of Athenian autochtony—which is why it is so important for Creusa to have an heir with Xuthus. However, after their marriage, Xuthus and Creusa are unable to have any children. At the end of the play, the birth of Dorus and Achaeus are promised to them by Apollo; but at the beginning of the play they remain childless, even though they desparately need children to endow Athens with dynastic continuity. And so both of them come to Delphi to ask Apollo if they shall ever have children. And so the play begins.

Apollo's Silence

But, of course, Creusa and Xuthus do not have exactly the same question to ask the god Apollo. Xuthus' question is very clear and simple: "I've never had children. Shall I have any with Creusa?" Creusa, however, has another question to ask. She must know whether she will ever have children with Xuthus. But she also wishes to ask: "With you, Apollo, I had a child. And I need to know now whether he is still living or not. What, Apollo, has become of our son?"

Apollo's temple, the oracle at Delphi, was the place where

the truth was told by the gods to any mortals who came to consult it. Both Xuthus and Creusa arrive together in front of the temple door and, of course, the first person they meet is Ion—Apollo's servant and son to Creusa. But naturally Creusa does not recognize her son, nor does Ion recognize his mother. They are strangers to one another, just as Oedipus and Jocasta were initially in Sophocles' *Oedipus the King*.

Remember that Oedipus was also saved from death in spite of the will of his mother. And he, too, was unable to recognize his real father and mother. The structure of *Ion*'s plot is somewhat similar to the Oedipus-story. But the dynamics of truth in the two plays are exactly reversed. For in *Oedipus the King*, Phoebus Apollo speaks the truth from the very beginning, truthfully foretelling what will happen. And human beings are the ones who continually hide from or avoid seeing the truth, trying to escape the destiny foretold by the god. But in the end, through the signs Apollo has given them, Oedipus and Jocasta discover the truth in spite of themselves. In the present play, human beings are trying to discover the truth: Ion wants to know who he is and where he comes from; Creusa wants to know the fate of her son. Yet it is Apollo who voluntarily *conceals* the truth. The Oedipal problem of truth is resolved by showing how mortals, in spite of their own blindness, will see the light of truth which is spoken by the god, and which they do not wish to see. The Ionic problem of truth is resolved by showing how human beings, in spite of the silence of Apollo, will discover the truth they are so eager to know.

The theme of god's silence prevails throughout *Ion*. It appears at the beginning of the tragedy when Creusa encounters Ion. Creusa is still ashamed of what happened to her, so she speaks to Ion as if she had come to consult the oracle for her "friend." She then tells him part of her own story, attributing it to her alleged friend, and asks him whether he thinks Apollo will give her friend an answer to her questions. As a good servant to the god, Ion tells her that Apollo will not give an answer. For if he has done what Creusa's friend claims, then he will be too ashamed:

> ION: …is Apollo to reveal what he intends should remain a mystery ?
> CREUSA: Surely his oracle is open for every Greek to question?
> ION: No. His honor is involved; you must respect his feelings.
> CREUSA: What of his victim's feelings? What does this involve for her?
> ION: There is no one who will ask this question for you. Suppose it were proved in Apollo's own temple that he had behaved so badly, he would be justified in making your interpreter suffer for it. My lady, let the matter drop. We must not accuse Apollo in his own court. That is what our folly would amount to, if we try to force a reluctant god to speak, to give signs in sacrifice or the flight of birds. Those ends we pursue against the gods' will can do us little good when we gain them…[25]

So at the very beginning of the play, Ion tells why Apollo will not tell the truth. And, in fact, he himself never answers Creusa's questions. This is a hiding-god.

What is even more significant and striking is what occurs at the end of the play when everything has been said by the

---

25. Euripides, *Ion*. Trans. Philip Velacott, lines 365–378.

various characters of the play, and the truth is known to everyone. For everyone then waits for Apollo's appearance—whose presence was not visible throughout the entire play (in spite of the fact that he is a main character in the dramatic events that unfold). It was traditional in ancient Greek tragedy for the god who constituted the main divine figure to appear last. Yet, at the end of the play Apollo—the shining god—does not appear. Instead, Athene arrives to convey his message. And she appears above the roof of the Delphic temple, for the temple doors are not open. Explaining why she has come, she says:

> ATHENE: ...I am your friend here as in Athens, the city whose name I bear—I am Athene! I have come in haste from Apollo. He thought it right not to appear to you himself, lest there be reproaches openly uttered for what is past; so he sends me with this message to you. Ion, this is your mother, and Apollo is your father. Xuthus did not beget you, but Apollo gave you to him so that you might become the recognized heir of an illustrious house. When Apollo's purpose in this matter was disclosed he contrived a way to save each of you from death at each other's hands. His intention has been to keep the truth secret for a while, and then in Athens to reveal Creusa as your mother, and you as her son by Apollo...[26]

So even at this final moment, when everything has come to light, Apollo does not dare to appear and speak the truth. He hides, while Athene speaks instead. We must remember that Apollo is the prophetic god in charge of speaking the

---

26. *Ibid.*, lines 1554–1568.

truth to mortals. Yet he is unable to play this role because he is ashamed of his guilt. Here, in *Ion*, silence and guilt are linked on the side of the god Apollo. In *Oedipus the King*, silence and guilt are linked on the side of mortals. The main motif of *Ion* concerns the human fight for truth against god's silence: human beings must manage, by themselves, to discover and to tell the truth. Apollo does not speak the truth, he does not reveal what he knows perfectly well to be the case, he deceives mortals by his silence or tells pure lies, he is not courageous enough to speak himself, and he uses his power, his freedom, and his superiority to cover up what he has done. Apollo is the *anti-parrhesiastes*.

In this struggle against the god's silence, Ion and Creusa are the two major parrhesiastic figures. But they do not play the role of the *parrhesiastes* in the same way. For as a male born of Athenian earth, Ion has the right to use *parrhesia*. Creusa, on the other hand, plays the parrhesiastic role as a woman who confesses her thoughts. I would like now to examine these two parrhesiastic roles, noting the nature of their difference.

Ion's Role

First, Ion. Ion's parrhesiastic role is evident in the very long scene which takes place between Ion and Xuthus early on in the play. When Xuthus and Creusa cme to consult the oracle, Xuthus enters the sanctuary first since he is the husband and the man. He asks Apollo his question, and the god tells him that the first person he meets when he comes out of the temple will be his son. And, of course, the first one he meets is Ion since, as Apollo's servant, he is always at the door of the temple. Here we have to pay attention to the Greek expression, which is not literally translated in either the French or English editions. The Greek words are:

παῖδ᾽ ἐμὸν πεφυκέναι.

The use of the word πεφυκέναι indicates that Ion is said to be Xuthus' son "by nature":

> ION: What was Apollo's oracle?
> XUTHUS: He said, whoever met me as I came out of the temple—
> ION: Whoever met you—yes: what about him?
> XUTHUS: —is my son! [παῖδ᾽ ἐμὸν πεφυκέναι].
> ION: Your son by birth, or merely by gift?
> XUTHUS: A gift, yes; but mine by birth too [δῶρον, ὄντα δ᾽ ἐζ ἐμοῦ].[27]

So you see that Apollo does not give an obscure and ambiguous oracular pronouncement as he was wont to do with indiscrete questioners. The god's answer is a pure lie. For Ion is *not* Xuthus' son "by nature" or "by birth." Apollo is not an ambiguous truth-teller in this case. He is a liar. And Xuthus, deceived by Apollo, candidly believes that Ion—the first person he meets—is really, by nature, his own son.

What follows is the first main parrhesiastic scene of the play, which can be divided into three parts.

The first part [ll. 517–527] concerns the *misunderstanding* between Ion and Xuthus. Xuthus leaves the temple, sees Ion, and—in light of Apollo's answer—believes that he is his son. Full of cheer, he goes to him and wants to kiss him [φίλημα, l. 519]. Ion—who does not know who Xuthus is, and does not know why he wants to kiss him—misunderstands Xuthus' behavior and thinks that Xuthus wants to have sex with him

---

27. *Ibid.*, lines 533–536.

(as any young Greek boy would if a man tried to kiss him). Most of the commentators, if they are even willing to recognize the sexual interpretation Ion attributes to Xuthus' behavior, say that this is a "comic scene"—which sometimes occurs in Euripides' tragedies. In any case, Ion says to Xuthus: "If you continue harassing me, I'll shoot an arrow in your chest." This is similar to *Oedipus the King,* where Oedipus does not know that Laius, King of Thebes, is his father. And he also misunderstands the nature of his encounter with him; a quarrel ensues, and Laius is killed by Oedipus. But in *Ion* there is this reversal: Xuthus, King of Athens, does not know that Ion is *not* his son, and Ion does not know that Xuthus thinks that he is Ion's father. So as a consequence of Apollo's lies we are in a world of deception.

The second part of this scene [ll. 528–562] concerns the *mistrust* of Ion towards Xuthus. Xuthus tells Ion: "Take it easy; if I want to kiss you, it is because I am your father." But rather than rejoicing at the discovery of knowing who his father is, Ion's first question to Xuthus is: "Who, then, is my mother?" [l. 539]. For some unknown reason, Ion's principal concern is the knowledge of his mother's identity. But then he asks Xuthus: "How can I be your son?" And Xuthus replies: "I don't know how; I refer you to the god Apollo for what he has said" [l. 543: οὐκ οἶδ', ἀναφέρω δ' εἰς τὸν θεόν]. Ion then utters a very interesting line which has been completely mistranslated in the French version. The Greek is [l. 544]:

φέρε λόγων ἀψώμεθ' ἄλλων.

The French edition translates as: "Come, let's speak about something else." A more accurate rendition might be: "Let us try another kind of discourse." So in answer to Ion's question of how he could be his son, Xuthus replies that he does not know, but was told as much by Apollo. And Ion tells him, in effect, then let's try another kind of discourse more capable of telling the truth:

> ION: How could I be yours?
> XUTHUS: Apollo, not I, has the answer.
> ION (after a pause): Let us try another tack [l. 544].
> XUTHUS: Yes, that will help us more.[28]

Abandoning the oracular formulation of the god, Xuthus and Ion take up an inquiry involving the exchange of questions and answers. As the inquirer, Ion questions Xuthus—his alleged father—to try to discover with whom, when, and how it was possible for him to have a child such that Ion might be his son. And Xuthus answers him: "Well, I think I had sex with a Delphian girl." When? "Before I was married to Creusa." Where? "Maybe in Delphi." How? "One day when I was drunk while celebrating the Dionysian torch feast." And of course, as an explanation of Ion's birth, this entire train of thought is pure baloney; but they take this inquisitive method seriously, and try, as best they can, to discover the truth by their own means—led as they are by Apollo's lies. Following this inquiry, Ion rather reluctantly and unenthusiastically accepts Xuthus' hypothesis: he considers himself to be Xuthus' son. The third part of the parrhesiastic scene between Xuthus and Ion concerns Ion's *political destiny,* and his potential political misfortunes if he arrives in Athens as the son and heir of Xuthus [ll. 563–675]. For after persuading Ion that he

---

28. Euripides, *Ion.* Trans. Ronald Frederick Willetts, lines 542–544.

is his son, Xuthus promises to bring Ion back to Athens
where, as the son of a king, he would be rich and powerful. But
Ion is not very enthusiastic about this prospect; for he knows
that he would be coming to Athens as the son of Xuthus (a foreigner to Athenian earth), and with an unknown mother. And
according to Athenian legislation, one cannot be a regular citizen in Athens if one is not the offspring of parents both of
whom were born in Athens. So Ion tells Xuthus that he would
be considered a foreigner and a bastard, i.e., a nobody. This
anxiety leads to a long development which at first glance
seems to be a digression, but which presents Euripides' critical portrayal of Athenian political life: both in a democracy
and concerning the political life of a monarch.

Ion explains that in a *democracy* there are three categories
of citizens [ll. 596–603]: (1) those who are called, using the
political vocabulary of the time, the ἀδύνατοι: those Athenian
citizens who have neither power nor wealth, and who hate all
who are superior to them; (2) those who are χρηστοὶ
δυνάμενοι: good Athenians who are capable of exercising
power, but because they are wise [σοφοί] they keep silent
[σιγῶσι] and do not worry about the political affairs of the city
[κοὐ σπεύδουσιυ εἰς τὰ πράγματα]; and finally (3) those rep-
utable men who are powerful, and use their discourse and reason to participate in public political life. Envisioning the reactions of these three groups to his appearance in Athens as a
foreigner and a bastard, Ion says that the first group, the
ἀδύνατοι, will hate him; the second group, the wise, will
laugh at the young man who wishes to be regarded as one of
the First Citizens of Athens; and the last group, the politi-
cians, will be jealous of their new competitor and will try to get
rid of him. So coming to a democratic Athens is not a cheerful
prospect for Ion.

Following this portrayal of democratic life, Ion speaks of the negative aspects of a family life with a step-mother who, herself childless, would not accept his presence as heir to the Athenian throne [ll. 608–620]. But then Ion returns to the political picture, giving his portrayal of the life of a monarch:

> ION: ...As for being a king, it is overrated. Royalty conceals a life of torment behind a pleasant facade. To live in hourly fear, looking over your shoulder for the assassin—is that paradise? Is it even good fortune? Give me the happiness of a plain man, not the life of a king, who loves to fill his court with criminals, and hates honest men for fear of death. You may tell me the pleasure of being rich outweighs everything. But to live surrounded by scandal, holding on to your money with both hands, beset by worry—has no appeal for me.[29]

These two descriptions of Athenian democratic life and the life of a monarch seem quite out of place in this scene, for Ion's problem is to discover who his mother is so as to arrive in Athens without shame or anxiety. We must find a reason for the inclusion of these two portrayals. The play continues and Xuthus tells Ion not to worry about his life in Athens, and for the time being proposes that Ion pretend to be a visiting houseguest and not disclose the "fact" that he is Xuthus' son. Later on, when a suitable time arrives, Xuthus proposes to make Ion his inheritor; but for now, nothing will be said to Creusa. Ion would like to come to Athens as the real successor to the second dynastic family of Erectheus, but what Xuthus

---

29 Euripides, *Ion*. Trans. Philip Vellacott, lines 621–632.

proposes—for him to pretend to be a visitor to the city—does not address Ion's real concerns. So the scene seems crazy, makes no sense. Nonetheless, Ion accepts Xuthus' proposal but claims that without knowing who his mother is, life will be impossible:

> ION: Yes, I will go. But one piece of good luck eludes me still: unless I find my mother, my life is worthless.[30]

Why is it impossible for Ion to live without finding his mother? He continues:

> ION: ...If I may do so, I pray my mother is Athenian, so that through her I may have rights of speech [παρρησία]. For when a stranger comes into the city of pure blood, though in name a citizen, his mouth remains a slave: he has no right of speech [παρρησία].[31]

So you see, Ion needs to know who his mother is so as to determine whether she is descended from the Athenian earth; for only thus will he be endowed with *parrhesia*. And he explains that someone who comes to Athens as a foreigner—even if he is literally and legally considered a citizen—still cannot enjoy *parrhesia*. What, then, does the seemingly digressive critical portrayals of democratic and monarchic life mean, culminating as they do in this final reference to *parrhesia* just when Ion accepts Xuthus' offer to return with him to Athens—especially given the rather obscure terms Xuthus proposes?

---

30. Euripides, *Ion.* Trans. Ronald Frederick Willetts, lines 668–670.
31. *Ibid.,* lines 670–675.

The digressive critical portrayals Ion gives of democracy and monarchy (or tyranny) are easy to recognize as typical instances of parrhesiastic discourse. For you can find almost exactly the same sorts of criticisms later on coming from Socrates' mouth in the works of either Plato or Xenophon. Similar critiques are given later by Isocrates. So the critical depiction of democratic and monarchic life as presented by Ion is part of the constitutional character of the parrhesiastic individual in Athenian political life at the end of the Fifth and the beginning of the Fourth Centuries. Ion is just such a *parrhesiastes*, i.e., the sort of individual who is so valuable to democracy or monarchy since he is courageous enough to explain either to the *demos* or to the king just what the short-comings of their life really are. Ion is a parrhesiastic individual and shows himself to be such both in these small digressive political critiques, as well as afterwards when he states that he needs to know whether his mother is an Athenian since he needs *parrhesia*. For despite the fact that it is in the nature of his character to be a *parrhesiastes*, he cannot legally or institutionally use this natural *parrhesia* with which he is endowed if his mother is not Athenian. *Parrhesia* is thus not a right given equally to all Athenian citizens, but only to those who are especially prestigious through their family and their birth. And Ion appears as a man who is, by nature, a parrhesiastic individual, yet who is, at the same time, deprived of the right of free speech.

And why is this parrhesiastic figure deprived of his parrhesiastic right? Because the god Apollo–the prophetic god whose duty it is to speak the truth to mortals—is not courageous enough to disclose *his* own faults and to act as a *parrhesiastes*. In order for Ion to conform to his nature and to play the parrhesiastic role in Athens, something more is needed which he lacks, but which will be given to him by the other parrhesiastic figure in the play, viz., his mother, Creusa. And Creusa *will* be able to tell him the truth, thus freeing her parrhesiastic son to *use* his natural *parrhesia*.

Creusa's Role

Creusa's parrhesiastic role in the play is quite different from Ion's; as a woman, Creusa will not use *parrhesia* to speak the truth about Athenian political life to the king, but rather to publicly accuse Apollo for his misdeeds.

When Creusa is told by the Chorus that Xuthus alone has been given a son by Apollo, she realizes that not only will she not find the son she is searching for, but also that when she returns to Athens she will have in her own home a step-son who is a foreigner to the city, yet who will nonetheless succeed Xuthus as king. And for these two reasons she is infuriated not only against her husband, but especially against Apollo. For after being raped by Apollo, and deprived by him of her son, to learn that now she will also not have her questions answered while Xuthus receives a son from the god—this proves to be too much for her to take. And her bitterness, her despair, and her anger bursts forth in an accusation made against Apollo: she decides to speak the truth. Truth thus comes to light as an emotional reaction to the god's injustice and his lies.

In Sophocles' *Oedipus the King,* mortals do not accept Apollo's prophetic utterances since their truth seems incredible; and yet they are led to the truth of the god's words in spite of their efforts to escape the fate that has been foretold by him. In Euripides' *Ion,* however, mortals are led to the truth in the face of the god's lies or silence, i.e., in spite of the fact that they are deceived by Apollo. As a consequence of Apollo's lies, Creusa believes that Ion is Xuthus' natural son. But in her emotional reaction to what she thinks is true, she ends up disclosing the truth.

Creusa's main parrhesiastic scene consists of two parts which differ in their poetic structure and in the type of *parrhesia* manifested. The first part takes the form of a beautiful long speech—a tirade against Apollo—while the second part is in the form of a *stichomythia*, a dialogue between Creusa and her servant consisting of alternate lines, one after the other.

First, the tirade. Creusa appears at this moment in front of the temple steps accompanied by an old man who is a trusted servant of the family (and who remains silent during Creusa's speech). Creusa's tirade against Apollo is that form of *parrhesia* where someone publicly accuses another of a crime, or of a fault or of an injustice that has been committed. And this accusation is an instance of *parrhesia* insofar as the one who is accused is more powerful than the one who accuses. For there is the danger that because of the accusation made, the accused may retaliate in some way against his or her accuser. So Creusa's *parrhesia* first takes the form of a public reproach or criticism against a being to whom she is inferior in power, and upon whom she is in a relation of dependence. It is in this vulnerable situation that Creusa decides to make her accusation:

CREUSA: O my heart, how be silent? Yet how can I speak of that secret love, strip myself of all shame? Is one barrier left still to prevent me? Whom have I now as my rival in virtue? Has not my husband become my betrayer? I am cheated of home, cheated of children, hopes are gone which I could not achieve, the hopes of arranging things well by hiding the facts, by hiding the birth which brought sorrow. No! No! But I swear by the starry abode of Zeus, by the goddess who reigns on our peaks and by

the sacred shore of the lake of Tritonis, I will no longer
conceal it: when I have put away the burden, my heart
will be easier. Tears fall from my eyes, and my spirit is
sick, evilly plotted against by men and gods; I will expose
them, ungrateful betrayers of women.

O you who give the seven-toned lyre a voice which
rings out of the lifeless, rustic horn the lovely sound of
the Muses' hymns, on you, Latona's son, here in daylight I
will lay blame. You came with hair flashing gold, as I
gathered into my cloak flowers ablaze with their golden
light. Clinging to my pale wrists as I cried for my mother's help you led me to bed in a cave, a god and my lover,
with no shame, submitting to the Cyprian's will. In mis-
ery I bore you a son, whom in fear of my mother I placed
in that bed where you cruelly forced me. Ah! He is lost
now, snatched as food for birds, my son and yours; O lost!
But you play the lyre, chanting your paeans.

O hear me, son of Latona, who assign your prophecies from the golden throne and the temple at the earth's
center, I will proclaim my words in your ears: you are an
evil lover; though you owed no debt to my husband, you
have set a son in his house. But my son, yes and yours,
hard-hearted, is lost, carried away by birds, the clothes
his mother put on him abandoned. Delos hates you and
the young laurel which grows by the palm with its deli-
cate leaves, where Latona bore you, a holy child, fruit of
Zeus.[32]

---

32. *Ibid.*, lines 859–922.

Regarding this tirade, I would like to emphasize the following three points: (1) As you can see, Creusa's accusation is
a public malediction against Apollo where, for example, the
references to Apollo as Latona's (Leto's) son are meant to convey the thought that Apollo was a bastard: the son of Latona
and Zeus. (2) There is also a clear metaphorical opposition
drawn between Phoebus Apollo as the god of light with his
golden brightness, who, at the same time, draws a young girl
into the darkness of a cave to rape her and is the son of
Latona—a divinity of the night, and so on. (3) And there is a
contrast drawn between the music of Apollo, with his seven-
chord lyre, and the cries and shouts of Creusa (who cries for
help as Apollo's victim, and who also must, through her shout-
ing malediction, speak the truth the god will not utter). For
Creusa delivers her accusations before the Delphic temple
doors—which are closed. The divine voice is silent while
Creusa proclaims the truth herself.

The second part of Creusa's parrhesiastic scene directly
follows this tirade when her old servant and guardian, who has
heard all that she has said, takes up an interrogative inquiry
which is exactly symmetrical to the stichomythic dialogue that
occurred between Ion and Xuthus. In the same way, Creusa's
servant asks her to tell him her story while he asks her questions such as when did these events happen, where, how, and
so on.

Two things are worthy of note about this exchange. First,
this interrogative inquiry is the reversal of the oracular disclosure of truth. Apollo's oracle is usually ambiguous and
obscure, never answers a set of precise questions directly, and
cannot proceed as an inquiry; whereas the method of question
and answer brings the obscure to light. Secondly, Creusa's parrhesiastic discourse is now no longer an accusation directed

towards Apollo, i.e., is no longer the accusation of a woman towards her rapist; but takes the form of a self-accusation where she reveals her own faults, weaknesses, misdeeds (exposing the child), and so forth. And Creusa confesses the events that transpired in a manner similar to Phaedra's confession of love for Hippolytus. For like Phaedra, she also manifests the same reluctance to say everything, and manages to let her servant pronounce those aspects of her story which she does not want to confess directly—employing a somewhat indirect confessional discourse which is familiar to everyone from Euripides' *Hippolytus* or Racine's *Phaedra*.

In any case, I think that Creusa's truth-telling is what we could call an instance of *personal* (as opposed to political) *parrhesia*. Ion's *parrhesia* takes the form of truthful political criticism, while Creusa's *parrhesia* takes the form of a truthful accusation against another more powerful than she, and as a confession of the truth about herself.

It is the combination of the parrhesiastic figures of Ion and Creusa which makes possible the full disclosure of truth at the end of the play. For following Creusa's parrhesiastic scene, no one except the god knows that the son Creusa had with Apollo is Ion, just as Ion does not know that Creusa is his mother and that he is not Xuthus' son. Yet to combine the two parrhesiastic discourses requires a number of other episodes which, unfortunately, we have no time now to analyze. For example, there is the very interesting episode where Creusa— still believing that Ion is Xuthus' natural son—tries to kill Ion; and when Ion discovers this plot, he tries to kill Creusa— a peculiar reversal of the Oedipal situation.

Regarding the schema we outlined, however, we can now see that the series of truths descended from Athens (Erectheus-Creusa-Ion) is complete at the end of the play. Xuthus, also, is deceived by Apollo to the end, for he returns to Athens still believing Ion is his natural son. And Apollo never appears anywhere in the play: he continually remains silent.

ORESTES [408 B.C.] [33]

A final occurrence of the word *parrhesia* can be found in Euripides' *Orestes,* a play written, or at least performed, in 408 B.C., just a few years before Euripides' death, and at a moment of political crisis in Athens when there were numerous debates about the democratic regime. This text is interesting because it is the only passage in Euripides where the word *parrhesia* is used in a pejorative sense. The word occurs on line 905 and is translated here as "ignorant outspokenness." The text in the play where the word appears is in the narrative of a messenger who has come to the royal palace at Argos to tell Electra what has happened in the Pelasgian court at Orestes' trial. For, as you know from *Electra,* Orestes and Electra have killed their mother, Clytemnestra, and thus are on trial for matricide. The narrative I wish to quote reads as follows:

> MESSENGER: …When the full roll of citizens was present, a herald stood up and said "Who wishes to address the court, to say whether or not Orestes ought to die for matricide?" At this Talthybius rose, who was your father's colleague in the victory over Troy. Always subservient to those in power, he made an ambiguous speech, with fulsome praise of Agamemnon and cold words for your

---

33. Third Lecture: 7 November 1983.

brother, twisting eulogy and censure both together—lay-
ing down a law useless to parents; and with every sentence gave ingratiating glances towards Aegisthus'
friends. Heralds are like that—their whole race have
learnt to jump to the winning side; their friend is anyone
who has power or a government office. Prince Diomedes
spoke up next. He urged them not to sentence either you
or your brother to death, but satisfy piety by banishing
you. Some shouted in approval; others disagreed.

Next there stood up a man with a mouth like a running spring, a giant in impudence, an enrolled citizen, yet
no Argive; a mere cat's-paw; putting his confidence in
bluster and ignorant outspokenness [παρρησία], and still
persuasive enough to lead his hearers into trouble. He
said you and Orestes should be killed with stones; yet, as
he argued for your death, the words he used were not his
own, but all prompted by Tyndareos.

Another rose, and spoke against him—one endowed
with little beauty, but a courageous man; the sort not
often found mixing in street or market-place, a manual
laborer—the sole backbone of the land; shrewd, when he
chose, to come to grips in argument; a man of blameless
principle and integrity.

He said, Orestes son of Agamemnon should be honored with crowns for daring to avenge his father by taking
a depraved and godless woman's life—one who corrupted
custom; since no man would leave his home, and arm
himself, and march to war, if wives left there in trust

---

34. Euripides, *Orestes*. Trans. Philip Vellacott, lines 884–931 [Lines considered an interpolation (in parentheses in the text) omitted].

could be seduced by stay-at-homes, and brave men cuckolded. His words seemed sensible to honest judges; and
there were no more speeches.[34]

As you can see, the narrative starts with a reference to the
Athenian procedure for criminal trials: when all the citizens
are present, a herald rises and cries "τίς χρήζει λέγειν"—
"Who wishes to speak?" [l. 885]. For that is the Athenian right
of equal speech (*isegoria*). Two orators then speak, both of
whom are borrowed from Greek mythology, from the Homeric
world. The first is Talthybius, who was one of Agamemnon's
companions during the war against the Trojans—specifically,
his herald. Talthybius is followed by Diomedes—one of the
most famous Greek heroes, known for his unmatched courage,
bravery, skill in battle, physical strength, and eloquence.

The messenger characterizes Talthybius as someone who
is not completely free, but dependent upon those more powerful than he is. The Greek text states that he is "ὑπὸ τοῖς
δυναμένοισιν ὤν…"—"under the power of the powerful"
("subservient to those in power") [l. 889]. There are two other
plays where Euripides criticizes this type of human being, the
herald. In *The Women of Troy*, the very same Talthybius appears
after the city of Troy has been captured by the Greek army to
tell Cassandra that she is to be the concubine of Agamemnon.
Cassandra gives her reply to the herald's news by predicting
that she will bring ruin to her enemies. And, as you know,
Cassandra's prophecies are always true. Talthybius, however,
does not believe her predictions. Since, as a herald, he does not
know what is true (he is unable to recognize the truth of
Cassandra's utterances), but merely repeats what his master—
Agamemnon—tells him to say, he thinks that Cassandra is
simply mad; for he tells her: "οὐ γὰρ ἀρτίας ἔχεις φρένας" —

"your mind is not in the right place" ("you're not in your right mind"). And to this Cassandra answers:

> CASSANDRA: "Servant"! You hear this servant? He's a herald. What are heralds, then, but creatures universally loathed—lackeys and menials to governments and kings? You say my mother is destined for Odysseus' home: what then of Apollo's oracles, spelt out to me, that she shall die here?[35]

And in fact, Cassandra's mother, Hecuba, dies in Troy.

In Euripides' *The Suppliant Women*, there is also a discussion between an unnamed herald (who comes from Thebes) and Theseus (who is not exactly the king, but the First Citizen of Athens) [ll. 399–463]. When the herald enters he asks, "Who is the King in Athens?" Theseus tells him that he will not be able to find the Athenian king since there is no *tyrannos* in the city:

> THESEUS: …This state is not subject to one man's will, but is a free city. The king here is the people, who by yearly office govern in turn. We give no special power to wealth; the poor man's voice commands equal authority.[36]

This sets off an argumentative discussion about which form of government is best: monarchy or democracy? The herald praises the monarchic regime, and criticizes democracy as subject to the whims of the rabble. Theseus' reply is in praise of the Athenian democracy where, because the laws are

---

35. Euripides, *The Women of Troy*. Trans. Philip Vellacott, lines 424–429
36. Euripides, *The Suppliant Women*. Trans. Philip Vellacott, lines 405–408.

written down, the poor and rich have equal rights, and where everyone is free to speak in the *ekklesia:*

> THESEUS: ...Freedom lives in this formula: "Who has good counsel which he would offer to the city?" He who desires to speak wins fame; he who does not is silent. Where could greater equality be found?[37]

The freedom to speak is thus synonymous with democratic equality in Theseus' eyes, which he cites in opposition to the herald—the representative of tyrannic power.

Since freedom resides in the freedom to speak the truth, Talthybius cannot speak directly and frankly at Orestes' trial since he is not free, but dependent upon those who are more powerful than he is. Consequently, he "speaks ambiguously" [λέγειν διχόμυθα], using a discourse which means two opposite things at the same time. So we see him praising Agamemnon (for he was Agamemnon's herald), but also condemning Agamemnon's son Orestes (since he does not approve of his actions). Fearful of the power of both factions, and therefore wishing to please everybody, he speaks two-facedly; but since Aegisthus' friends have come to power, and are calling for Orestes' death (Aegisthus, you remember from *Electra*, was also killed by Orestes), in the end Talthybius condemns Orestes.

Following this negative mythological character is a positive one: Diomedes. Diomedes was famous as a Greek warrior both for his courageous exploits and for his noble eloquence: his skill in speaking, and his wisdom. Unlike Talthybius,

---

37. *Ibid.,* lines 438–442.

Diomedes is independent; he says what he thinks, and proposes a moderate solution which has no political motivation: it is not a revengeful retaliation. On religious grounds, "to satisfy piety," he urges that Orestes and Electra be exiled to purify the country of Clytemnestra's and Aegisthus' deaths according to the traditional religious punishment for murder. But despite Diamedes' moderate and reasonable verdict, his opinion divides the assembly: some agree, others disagree.

We then have two other speakers who present themselves. Their names are not given, they do not belong to the mythological world of Homer, they are not heroes; but from the precise description which the reporting messenger gives of them, we can see that they are two "social types." The first one (who is symmetrical to Talthybius, the bad orator) is the sort of orator who is so harmful for a democracy. And I think we should determine carefully his specific characteristics.

His first trait is that he has "a mouth like a running spring"—which translates the Greek word *athuroglossos* [ἀθὑρογλωσσος]. *Athuroglossos* comes from γλῶδσα (tongue) and θύρα (door); it thus literally refers to someone who has a tongue but not a door. Hence it implies someone who cannot shut his mouth.

The metaphor of the mouth, teeth, and lips as a door that is closed when one is silent occurs frequently in ancient Greek literature. In the Sixth Century B.C., for example, Theognis writes in his *Elegies* that there are too many garrulous people:

> Too many tongues have gates which fly apart
> Too easily, and care for many things
> That don't concern them. Better to keep bad news
> Indoors, and only let the good news out.[38]

In the Second Century A.D., in his essay "Concerning Talkativeness" [Περὶ ἀδολεσχίας], Plutarch also writes that the teeth are a fence or gate such that "if the tongue does not obey or restrain itself, we may check its incontinence by biting it till it bleeds."[39]

This notion of being *athuroglossos*, or of being *athurostomia* [ἀθὺροστομία] (one who has a mouth without a door), refers to someone who is an endless babbler, who cannot keep quiet, and is prone to say whatever comes to mind. Plutarch compares the talkativeness of such people with the Black Sea—which has neither doors nor gates to impede the flow of its waters into the Mediterranean:

> ...those who believe that storerooms without doors and purses without fastenings are of no use to their owners, yet keep their mouths without lock or door, maintaining as perpetual an outflow as the mouth of the Black Sea, appear to regard speech [λόγος] as the least valuable of all things. They do not, therefore, meet with belief, which is the object of all speech.[40]

As you can see, *athuroglossos* is characterized by the following two traits: (1) When you have "a mouth like a running spring," you cannot distinguish those occasions when you should speak from those when you should remain silent; or that which must be said from that which must remain unsaid; or the circumstances and situations where speech is required from those where one ought to remain silent. Thus Theognis

---

38. Theognis, *Elegies.* Trans. Dorothea Wender, lines 421–424.
39. Plutarch, "Concerning Talkativeness." Trans. W. C. Helmbold, 503c.
40. *Ibid.*

states that garrulous people are unable to differentiate when one should give voice to good or bad news, or how to demarcate their own from other people's affairs—since they indiscretely intervene in the cares of others. (2) As Plutarch notes, when you are *athuroglossos* you have no regard for the value of *logos,* for rational discourse as a means of gaining access to truth. *Athuroglossos* is thus almost synonymous with *parrhesia* taken in its pejorative sense, and exactly the opposite of *parrhesia*'s positive sense (since it is a sign of wisdom to be able to use *parrhesia* without falling into the garrulousness of *athuroglossos).* One of the problems which the parrhesiastic character must resolve, then, is how to distinguish that which must be said from that which should be kept silent. For not everyone can draw such a distinction, as the following example illustrates.

In his treatise "The Education of Children" [Περὶ παίδων ἀγωγῆς], Plutarch gives an anecdote of Theocritus, a sophist, as an example of *athuroglossos* and of the misfortunes incurred by intemperate speech. The king of the Macedonians, Antigonus, sent a messenger to Theocritus asking him to come to his court to engage in discussion. And it so happened that the messenger he sent was his chief cook, Eutropian. King Antigonus had lost an eye in battle, so he was one-eyed. Now Theocritus was not pleased to hear from Eutropian, the king's cook, that he had to go and visit Antigonus; so he said to the cook: "I know very well that you want to serve me up raw to your Cyclops"[41]—thus subjecting the king's disfigurement and Eutropian's profession to ridicule. To which the cook replied: "Then you shall not keep your head on, but you

---

41. Plutarch, "The Education of Children." Trans. F. C. Babbitt, 11c.

shall pay the penalty for this reckless talk [*athurostomia*] and madness of yours."[42] And when Eutropian reported Theocritus' remark to the king, he sent and had Theocritus put to death.

As we shall see in the case of Diogenes, a really fine and courageous philosopher *can* use *parrhesia* towards a king; however, in Theocritus' case his frankness is not *parrhesia* but *athurostomia* since to joke about a king's disfigurement or a cook's profession has no noteworthy philosophical significance. *Athuroglossos* or *athurostomia*, then, is the first trait of the third orator in the narration of Orestes' trial.

His second trait is that he is "ἰσχύων θράσει"—"a giant in impudence" [l. 903]. The word ἰσχύω denotes someone's strength, usually the physical strength which enables one to overcome others in competition. So this speaker is strong, but he is strong "θράσει" which means strong not because of his reason, or his rhetorical ability to speak, or his ability to pronounce the truth, but only because he is arrogant. He is strong only by his bold arrogance.

A third characteristic: "an enrolled citizen, yet no Argive." He is not native to Argos, but comes from elsewhere and has been integrated into the city. The expression ἠναγκασμένος [l. 904] refers to someone who has been imposed upon the members of the city as a citizen by force or by dishonorable means [what gets translated as "a mere cat's paw"].

His fourth trait is given by the phrase "θορύβῳ τε πίσυνος"—"putting his confidence in bluster." He is confident in *thorubos* [θόρυβος], which refers to the noise made by a strong voice, by a scream, a clamor, or uproar. When, for instance, in battle, the soldiers scream in order to bring forth

---

42. *Ibid.*

their own courage or to frighten the enemy, the Greeks used the word *thorubos*. Or the tumultuous noise of a crowded assembly when the people shouted was called *thorubos*. So the third orator is not confident in his ability to formulate articulate discourse, but only in his ability to generate an emotional reaction from his audience by his strong and loud voice. This direct relationship between the voice and the emotional effect it produces on the *ekklesia* is thus opposed to the rational sense of articulate speech. The final characteristic of the third (negative) speaker is that he also puts his confidence in "κάμθει παρρησία"—"ignorant outspokenness [*parrhesia*]." The phrase "κάμθει παρρησία" repeats the expression *athuroglossos*, but with its political implications. For although this speaker has been imposed upon the citizenry, he nonetheless possesses *parrhesia* as a formal civic right guaranteed by the Athenian constitution. What designates his *parrhesia* as *parrhesia* in its pejorative or negative sense, however, is that it lacks *mathesis* [μάθησις]—learning or wisdom. In order for *parrhesia* to have positive political effects, it must now be linked to a good education, to intellectual and moral formation, to *paideia* or *mathesis*. Only then will *parrhesia* be more than *thorubos* or sheer vocal noise. For when speakers use *parrhesia* without *mathesis*, when they use "κάμθει παρρησία," the city is led into terrible situations.

You may recall a similar remark of Plato's, in his Seventh Letter [336b], concerning the lack of *mathesis*. There Plato explains that Dion was not able to succeed with his enterprise in Sicily (viz., to realize in Dionysius both a ruler of a great city and a philosopher devoted to reason and justice) for two reasons. The first is that some *daimon* or evil spirit may have been jealous and wanted vengence. And secondly, Plato explains that ignorance [ἀμαθία] broke out in Sicily. And of ἀμαθία Plato says that it is "the soil in which all manner of evil to all men takes root and flourishes and later produces a fruit most bitter for those who sowed it."[43]

The characteristics, then, of the third speaker—a certain social type who employs *parrhesia* in its pejorative sense—are these: he is violent, passionate, a foreigner to the city, lacking in *mathesis,* and therefore dangerous.

And now we come to the fourth and final speaker at Orestes' trial. He is analogous to Diomedes: what Diomedes was in the Homeric world, this last orator is in the political world of Argos. An exemplification of the positive *parrhesiastes* as a "social type," he has the following traits.

The first is that he is "one endowed with little beauty, but a courageous man" [μορφῇ μὲν οὐκ ευωπός ἀνδρεῖος δ' ἀνήρ] [l. 918]. Unlike a woman, he is not fair to look at, but a "manly man," i.e., a courageous man. Euripides is playing on the etymology of the word ἀνδρεία (manliness or courage), which comes from the word ἀνήρ. Ἀνήρ means "man" (understood as the opposite of "woman" and not as the opposite of "beast"). For the Greeks, courage is a virile quality which women were said not to possess.

Secondly, he is "the sort not often found mixing in street or marketplace [ἀγορά]" [l. 919]. So this representative of the positive use of *parrhesia* is not the sort of professional politician who spends most of his time in the *agora*—the place where the people, the assembly, met for political discussion and debate. Nor is he one of those poor persons who, without any other means to live by, would come to the *agora* in order to receive the sums of money given to those taking part in the

43. Plato, *Letters* (VII). Trans. L. A. Post, 336b. Cf. *Laws,* 688c.

ekklesia. He takes part in the assembly only to participate in important decisions at critical moments. He does not live off of politics for politics' sake.

Thirdly, he is an *"autourgos"* [αὐτουργός]—"a manual laborer" [l. 920]. The word *autourgos* refers to someone who works his own land. The word denotes a specific social category—neither the great landowner nor the peasant, but the landowner who lives and works with his own hands on his own estate, occasionally with the help of a few servants or slaves. Such landowners—who spent most of their time working the fields and supervising the work of their servants—were highly praised by Xenophon in his *Oeconomicus.*[44] What is most interesting in *Orestes* is that Euripides emphasizes the political competence of such landowners by mentioning three aspects of their character.

The first is that they are always willing to march to war and fight for the city, which they do better than anyone else. Of course, Euripides does not give any rational explanation of why this should be so; but if we refer to Xenophon's *Oeconomicus* where the *autourgos* is depicted, there are a number of reasons given.[45] A major explanation is that the landowner who works his own land is, naturally, very interested in the defense and protection of the lands of the country—unlike the shopkeepers and the people living in the city who do not own their own land, and hence do not care as much if the enemy pillages the countryside. But those who work as farmers simply cannot tolerate the thought that the enemy might ravage the farms, burn the crops, kill the flocks and herds, and so on; and hence they make good fighters.

---

44. Cf. Xenophon, *Oeconomicus.* Trans. Carnes Lord, Chapter V.
45. *Ibid.,* Chapter XXI.

Secondly, the *autourgos* is able "to come to grips in argument" [l. 921], i.e., is able to use language to propose good advice for the city. As Xenophon explains, such landowners are used to giving orders to their servants, and making decisions about what must be done in various circumstances. So not only are they good soldiers, they also make good leaders. Hence when they do speak to the *ekklesia*, they do not use *thorubos*; but what they say is important, reasonable, and constitutes good advice.

In addition, the last orator is a man of moral integrity: "a man of blameless principle and integrity" [l. 922].

A final point about the *autourgos* is this: whereas the previous speaker wanted Electra and Orestes to be put to death by stoning, not only does this landowner call for Orestes' acquittal, he believes Orestes should be "honored with crowns" for what he has done. To understand the significance of the *autourgos'* statement, we need to realize that what is at issue in Orestes' trial for the Athenian audience—living in the midst of the Peloponnesian War—is the question of war or peace: will the decision concerning Orestes be an aggressive one that will institute the continuation of hostilities, as in war, or will the decision institute peace? The *autourgos'* proposal of an acquittal symbolizes the will for peace. But he also states that Orestes should be crowned for killing Clytemnestra "since no man would leave his home, and arm himself, and march to war, if wives left there in trust could be seduced by stay-at-homes, and brave men cuckolded" [ll. 925–929]. We must remember that Agamemnon was murdered by Aegisthus just after he returned home from the Trojan War; for while he was fighting the enemy away from home, Clytemnestra was living in adultery with Aegisthus.

And now we can see the precise historical and political

context for this scene. The year of the play's production is 408 B.C., a time when the competition between Athens and Sparta in the Peloponnesian War was still very sharp. The two cities have been fighting now for twenty-three long years, with short intermittent periods of truce. Athens in 408 B.C., following several bitter and ruinous defeats in 413, had recovered some of its naval power. But on land the situation was not good, and Athens was vulnerable to Spartan invasion. Nonetheless, Sparta made several offers of peace to Athens, so that the issue of continuing the war or making peace was vehemently discussed.

In Athens the democratic party was in favor of war for economic reasons which are quite clear; for the party was generally supported by merchants, shop-keepers, businessmen, and those who were interested in the imperialistic expansion of Athens. The conservative aristocratic party was in favor of peace since they gained their support from the landowners and others who wanted a peaceful co-existence with Sparta, as well as an Athenian constitution which was closer, in some respects, to the Spartan constitution.

The leader of the democratic party was Cleophon—who was not native to Athens, but a foreigner who registered as a citizen. A skillful and influential speaker, he was infamously portrayed in his life by his own contemporaries (for example, it was said he was not courageous enough to became a soldier, that he apparently played the passive role in his sexual relations with other men, and so on). So you see that all of the characteristics of the third orator, the negative *parrhesiastes*, can be attributed to Cleophon.

The leader of the conservative party was Theramenes— who wanted to return to a Sixth-Century Athenian constitution that would institute a moderate oligarchy. Following his proposal, the main civil and political rights would have been reserved for the landowners. The traits of the *autourgos,* the positive *parrhesiastes,* thus correspond to Theramenes.[47]

So one of the issues clearly present in Orestes' trial is the question that was then being debated by the democratic and conservative parties about whether Athens should continue the war with Sparta, or opt for peace.

PROBLEMATIZING *PARRHESIA*

In Euripides' *Ion,* written ten years earlier than *Orestes,* around 418 B.C., *parrhesia* was presented as having only a positive sense or value. And, as we saw, it was both the freedom to speak one's mind, and a privilege conferred on the first citizens of Athens—a privilege which Ion wished to enjoy. The *parrhesiastes* spoke the truth precisely because he was a good citizen, was well-born, had a respectful relation to the city, to the law, and to truth. And for Ion, the problem was that in order for him to assume the parrhesiastic role which came naturally to him, the truth about his birth had to be disclosed. But because Apollo did not wish to reveal this truth, Creusa had to disclose his birth by using *parrhesia* against the god in a public accusation. And thus Ion's *parrhesia* was established, was grounded in Athenian soil, in the game between the gods

---

47. According to Foucault's scheme, the succession of speakers may be placed as follows:

	Parrhesia	
	NEGATIVE SENSE	POSITIVE SENSE
Mythological Figures:	Talthybius	Diomedes
Politico-Social Types:	*amathes parrhesiastes*	*autourgos*
Political Figures Implied:	[Cleophon]	[Theramenes]

and mortals. So there was no "problematization" of the *parrhe-siastes* as such within this first conception.

In *Orestes*, however, there is a split within *parrhesia* itself between its positive and negative senses; and the problem of *parrhesia* occurs solely within the field of human parrhesiastic roles. This crisis of the *function* of *parrhesia* has two major aspects.

The first concerns the question: who is entitled to use *par-rhesia*? Is it enough simply to accept *parrhesia* as a civil right such that any and every citizen can speak in the assembly if and when he wishes? Or should *parrhesia* be exclusively grant-ed to some citizens only, according to their social status or per-sonal virtues? There is a discrepancy between an egalitarian system which enables everyone to use *parrhesia*, and the neces-sity of choosing among the citizenry those who are able (because of their social or personal qualities) to use *parrhesia* in such a way that it truly benefits the city. And this discrepancy generates the emergence of *parrhesia* as a problematic issue. For unlike *isonomia* (the equality of all citizens in front of the law) and *isegoria* (the legal right given to everyone to speak his own opinion), *parrhesia* was not clearly defined in institution-al terms. There was no law, for example, protecting the *parrhe-siastes* from potential retaliation or punishment for what he said. And thus there was also a problem in the relation between *nomos* and *aletheia*: how is it possible to give legal form to someone who relates to truth? There are formal laws of valid reasoning, but no social, political, or institutional laws determining who is able to *speak* the truth.

The second aspect of the crisis concerning the function of *parrhesia* has to do with the relation of *parrhesia* to *mathesis*, to knowledge and education—which means that *parrhesia* in and of itself is no longer considered adequate to disclose the truth.

The *parrhesiastes'* relation to truth can no longer simply be established by pure frankness or sheer courage, for the relation now requires education or, more generally, some sort of personal training. But the precise sort of personal training or education needed is also an issue (and is contemporaneous with the problem of sophistry). In *Orestes*, it seems more likely that the *mathesis* required is not that of the Socratic or Platonic conception, but the kind of experience that an *autourgos* would get through his own life.

And now I think we can begin to see that the crisis regarding *parrhesia* is a problem of truth: for the problem is one of recognizing who is capable of speaking the truth within the limits of an institutional system where everyone is equally entitled to give his own opinion. Democracy by itself is not able to determine who has the specific qualities which enable him to speak the truth (and thus should possess the right to tell the truth). And *parrhesia*, as a verbal activity, as pure frankness in speaking, is also not sufficient to disclose truth since negative *parrhesia*, ignorant outspokenness, can also result.

The crisis of *parrhesia*, which emerges at the crossroads of an interrogation about democracy and an interrogation about truth, gives rise to a *problematization* of some hitherto unproblematic relations between freedom, power, democracy, education, and truth in Athens at the end of the Fifth Century. From the previous problem of gaining *access* to *parrhesia* in spite of the silence of god, we move to a problematization of *parrhesia*, i.e., *parrhesia* itself becomes problematic, split within itself.

I do not wish to imply that *parrhesia*, as an explicit notion, emerges at this moment of crisis—as if the Greeks did not have any coherent idea of the freedom of speech previously, or of the value of free speech. What I mean is that there is a new problematization of the relations between verbal activity, education, freedom, power, and the existing political institutions which marks a crisis in the way freedom of speech is understood in Athens. And this problematization demands a new way of taking care of and asking questions about these relations.

I emphasize this point for at least the following methodological reason. I would like to distinguish between the "history of ideas" and the "history of thought." Most of the time a historian of ideas tries to determine when a specific concept appears, and this moment is often identified by the appearance of a new word. But what I am attempting to do as a historian of thought is something different. I am trying to analyze the way institutions, practices, habits, and behavior become a problem for people who behave in specific sorts of ways, who have certain types of habits, who engage in certain kinds of practices, and who put to work specific kinds of institutions. The history of ideas involves the analysis of a notion from its birth, through its development, and in the setting of other ideas which constitute its context. The history of thought is the analysis of the way an unproblematic field of experience, or a set of practices, which were accepted without question, which were familiar and "silent," out of discussion, becomes a problem, raises discussion and debate, incites new reactions, and induces a crisis in the previously silent behavior, habits, practices, and institutions. The history of thought, understood in this way, is the history of the way people begin to take care of something, of the way they become anxious about this or that—for example, about madness, about crime, about sex, about themselves, or about truth.

3.
Parrhesia in the Crisis of Democratic Institutions [48]

Today I would like to complete what I began last time about *parrhesia* and the crisis of democratic institutions in the Fourth Century B.C.; and then I would like to move on to the analysis of another form of *parrhesia*, viz., *parrhesia* in the field of personal relations (to oneself and to others), or *parrhesia* and the care of the self.

The explicit criticism of speakers who utilized *parrhesia* in its negative sense became a commonplace in Greek political thought after the Peloponnesian War; and a debate emerged concerning the relationship of *parrhesia* to democratic institutions.[49] The problem, very roughly put, was the following. Democracy is founded by a *politeia*, a constitution, where the *demos*, the people, exercise power, and where everyone is equal in front of the law. Such a constitution, however, is condemned to give equal place to all forms of *parrhesia*, even the worst. Because *parrhesia* is given even to the worst citizens, the overwhelming influence of bad, immoral, or ignorant speakers may lead the citizenry into tyranny, or may otherwise endanger the city. Hence *parrhesia* may be dangerous for democracy itself. To us this problem seems coherent and familiar, but for the Greeks the discovery of this problem, of a necessary antinomy between *parrhesia*—freedom of speech—and democracy, inaugurated a long impassioned debate concerning the precise nature of the dangerous relations which seemed to exist between democracy, *logos*, freedom, and truth.

We must take into account the fact that we know one side of the discussion much better than the other for the simple

---

48. Fourth Lecture: 14 November 1983.
49. Cf. Robert J. Jonner, *Aspects of Athenian Democracy,* 1933 (Chapter IV: "Freedom of Speech"); A.H.M. Jones, "The Athenian Democracy and its Critics" in *Athenian Democracy,* 1957: 41–72; Giuseppe Scarpat, *Parrhesia,* 38–57.

reason that most of the texts which have been preserved from this period come from writers who were either more or less directly affiliated with the aristocratic party, or at least distrustful of democratic or radically democratic institutions. And I would like to quote a number of these texts as examples of the problem we are examining.

The first one I would like to quote is an ultra-conservative, ultra-aristocratic lampooning of the democratic Athenian constitution, probably written during the second half of the Fifth Century. For a long time this lampoon was attributed to Xenophon. But now scholars agree that this attribution was not correct, and the Anglo-American classicists even have a nice nickname for this Pseudo-Xenophon, the unnamed author of this lampoon. They call him the "Old Oligarch." This text must came from one of those aristocratic circles or political clubs which were so active in Athens at the end of the Fifth Century. Such circles were very influential in the anti-democratic revolution of 411 B.C. during the Peloponnesian War.

The lampoon takes the form of a paradoxical praise or eulogy—a genre very familiar to the Greeks. The writer is supposed to be an Athenian democrat who focuses on some of the most obvious imperfections, shortcomings, blemishes, failures, etc., of Athenian democratic institutions and political life; and he praises these imperfections as if they were qualities with the most positive consequences. The text is without any real literary value since the writer is more aggressive than witty. But the main thesis which is at the root of most criticisms of Athenian democratic institutions can be found in this text, and is, I think, significant for this type of radically aristocratic attitude.

This aristocratic thesis is the following. The *demos,* the

people, are the most numerous. Since they are the most
numerous, the *demos* is also comprised of the most ordinary,
and indeed, even the worst, citizens. Therefore the *demos* cannot be comprised of the best citizens. And so what is best for
the *demos* cannot be what is best for the *polis*, for the city. With
this general argument as a background, the "Old Oligarch"
ironically praises Athenian democratic institutions; and there
are same lengthy passages caricaturing freedom of speech:

> Now one might say that the right thing would be that [the
> people] not allow all to speak on an equal footing, nor
> to have a seat in the council, but only the cleverest men
> and the best. But on this point, too, they have determined
> on the perfectly right thing by also allowing the vulgar
> people to speak. For if only the aristocracy were allowed
> to speak and took part in the debate, it would be good to
> them and their peers, but not to the proletarians. But now
> that any vulgar person who wants to do so may step for-
> ward and speak, he will just express that which is good to
> him and his equals.

> One might ask: How should such a person be able to
> understand what is good to him or to the people? Well,
> the masses understand that this man's ignorance, vulgar-
> ity, and sympathy are more useful to them than all the
> morals, wisdom, and antipathy of the distinguished man.
> With such a social order, it is true, a state will not be able
> to develop into perfection itself, but democracy will be
> best maintained in this manner. For the people do not
> want to be in the circumstances of slaves in a state with
> an ideal constitution, but to be free and be in power;
> whether the constitution is bad or no, they do not care

very much. For what you think is no ideal constitution, is just the condition for the people being in power and being free.

For if you seek an ideal constitution you will see that in the first place the laws are made by the most skillful persons; further the aristocracy will consult about the affairs of the state and put a stop to unruly persons having a seat in the council or speaking or taking part in the assembly of the people. But the people, well, they will as a consequence of these good reforms rather sink into slavery.[50]

Now I would like to switch to another text which presents a much more moderate position. It is a text written by Isocrates in the middle of the Fourth Century; and Isocrates refers several times to the notion of *parrhesia* and to the problem of free speech in a democracy. At the beginning of his great oration, "On the Peace" [Περὶ εἰρήνης], written in 355 B.C., Isocrates contrasts the Athenian people's attitude towards receiving advice about their private business when they consult reasonable, well-educated individuals with the way they consider advice when dealing with public affairs and political activities:

...whenever you take counsel regarding your private business you seek out as counsellors men who are your superiors in intelligence, but whenever you deliberate on the business of the state you distrust and dislike men of that

---

50. Pseudo-Xenophon, *The Constitution of the Athenians*. Trans. Hartvig Frisch, §§6–9.

character and cultivate, instead, the most depraved of the orators who come before you on this platform; and you prefer as being better friends of the people those who are drunk to those who are sober, those who are witless to those who are wise, and those who dole out the public money to those who perform public services at their own expense. So that we may well marvel that anyone can expect a state which employs such counsellors to advance to better things.[51]

But not only do Athenians listen to the most depraved orators; they are not even willing to hear truly good speakers, for they deny them the possibility of being heard:

I observe...that you do not hear with equal favor the speakers who address you, but that, while you give your attention to some, in the case of others you do not even suffer their voice to be heard. And it is not surprising that you do this; for in the past you have formed the habit of driving all the orators from the platform except those who support your desires.[52]

------

51. Isocrates, "On the Peace." Trans. George Norlin, §113. In his "Third Philippic" [341 B.C.], Demosthenes similarly remarks: "In other matters you think it so necessary to grant general freedom of speech [*parrhesia*] to everyone in Athens that you even allow aliens and slaves to share in the privilege, and many menials may be observed among you speaking their minds with more liberty than citizens enjoy in other states; but from your deliberations you have banished it utterly. Hence the result is that in the Assembly your self-complacency is flattered by hearing none but pleasant speeches, but your policy and your practice are already involving you in the gravest perils" [Trans. J.H. Vince; §§ 3–4].
52. Isocrates, "On the Peace," §3.

And that, I think, is important. For you see that the difference between the good and the bad orator does not lie primarily in the fact that one gives good while the other gives bad
advice. The difference lies in this: the depraved orators, who
are accepted by the people, only say what the people desire to
hear. Hence, Isocrates calls such speakers "flatterers"
[κόλακες]. The honest orator, in contrast, has the ability, and
is courageous enough, to oppose the *demos*. He has a critical
and pedagogical role to play which requires that he attempt to
transform the will of the citizens so that they will serve the
best interests of the city. This opposition between the people's
will and the city's best interests is fundamental to Isocrates'
criticism of the democratic institutions of Athens. And he
concludes that because it is not even possible to be heard in
Athens if one does not parrot the *demos'* will, there is democracy—which is a good thing—but the only parrhesiastic or
outspoken speakers left who have an audience are "reckless
orators" and "comic poets":

> ...I know that it is hazardous to oppose your views and
> that, although this is a free government, there exists no
> "freedom of speech" [*parrhesia*] except that which is
> enjoyed in this Assembly by the most reckless orators,
> who care nothing for your welfare, and in the theatre by
> the comic poets.[53]

---

53. Isocrates, "On the Peace." Trans. George Norlin, §14. Of comic *parrhesia* Werner Jaeger writes: "Comedy was produced by democracy as an anti-
dote to its own overdose of liberty, thereby outdoing its own excesses, and
extending *parrhesia*, its vaunted freedom of speech, to subjects which are
usually tabu even in a free political system... Comedy was the censorship
of Athens" [*Paideia*, Vol. 1. Trans. Gilbert Highet; 364–365].

Hence, real *parrhesia*, *parrhesia* in its positive, critical sense, does not exist where democracy exists.

In the "Areopagiticus" [355 B.C.], Isocrates draws a set of distinctions which similarly expresses this general idea of the incompatibility of true democracy and critical *parrhesia*. For he compares the old Solonian and Cleisthenean constitutions to present Athenian political life, and praises the older polities on the grounds that they gave to Athens democracy [δημοκρατία], liberty [ἐλευθερία], happiness [εὐδαιμονία], and equality in front of the law [ἰςονομία]. All of these positive features of the old democracy, however, he claims have become perverted in the present Athenian democracy. Democracy has become lack of self-restraint [ἀκολασία]; liberty has become lawlessness [παρανομία]; happiness has become the freedom to do whatever one pleases [ἐξουςία τοῦ πάντα ποιεῖν]; and equality in front of the law has become *parrhesia*.[54] *Parrhesia* in this text has only a negative, pejorative sense. So, as you can see, in Isocrates there is a constant positive evaluation of democracy in general, but coupled with the assertion that it is impossible to enjoy both democracy and *parrhesia* (understood in its positive sense). Moreover, there is the same distrust of the *demos'* feelings, opinions, and desires which we encountered, in more radical form, in the Old Oligarch's lampoon.

A third text I would like to examine comes from Plato's *Republic* [Book VIII, 557a–b], where Socrates explains how democracy arises and develops. For he tells Adeimantus that:

> When the poor win, the result is democracy. They kill some of the opposite party, banish others, and grant the

---

54. Isocrates, "Areopagiticus." Trans. George Norlin, §20.

rest an equal share in civil rights and government, offi-
cials being usually appointed by lot.[55]

Socrates then asks: "What is the character of this new
regime?" And he says of the people in a democracy:

> First of all, they are free. Liberty and free speech [*parrhe-
> sia*] are rife everywhere; anyone is allowed to do what he
> likes... That being so, every man will arrange his own
> manner of life to suit his pleasure.[56]

What is interesting about this text is that Plato does not
blame *parrhesia* for endowing everyone with the possibility of
influencing the city, including the worst citizens. For Plato,
the primary danger of *parrhesia* is not that it leads to bad decisions in government, or provides the means for some ignorant
or corrupt leader to gain power, to become a tyrant. The primary danger of liberty and free speech in a democracy is what
results when everyone has his own manner of life, his own
style of life, or what Plato calls "κατασκευή τοῦ βίου." For
then there can be no common *logos*, no possible unity, for the
city. Following the Platonic principle that there is an analogous relation between the way a human being behaves and the
way a city is ruled, between the hierarchical organization of
the faculties of a human being and the constitutional make-up
of the *polis*, you can see very well that if everyone in the city
behaves just as he wishes, with each person following his own
opinion, his own will or desires, then there are in the city as
many constitutions, as many small autonomous cities, as there

---

55. Plato, *Republic*. Trans. F. M. Cornford. Book VIII, 557a.
56. *Ibid.*, 557b.

are citizens doing whatever they please. And you can see that Plato also considers *parrhesia* not only as the freedom to say whatever one wishes, but as linked with the freedom to *do* whatever one wants. It is a kind of anarchy involving the freedom to choose one's own style of life without limit.

Well, there are numerous other things to say about the political problematization of *parrhesia* in Greek culture, but I think that we can observe two main aspects of this problematization during the Fourth Century.

First, as is clear in Plato's text for example, the problem of the freedom of speech becomes increasingly related to the choice of existence, to the choice of one's way of life. Freedom in the use of *logos* increasingly becomes freedom in the choice of *bios*. And as a result, *parrhesia* is regarded more and more as a personal attitude, a personal quality, as a virtue which is useful for the city's political life in the case of positive or critical *parrhesia*, or as a danger for the city in the case of negative, pejorative *parrhesia*.

In Demosthenes, for example, one can find a number of references to *parrhesia*;[57] but *parrhesia* is usually spoken of as a personal quality, and not as an institutional right. Demosthenes does not seek or make an issue of institutional guarantees for *parrhesia*, but insists on the fact that he, as a personal citizen, will use *parrhesia* because he must boldly speak the truth about the city's bad politics. And he claims that in so doing, he runs a great risk. For it is dangerous for him to speak freely, given that the Athenians in the Assembly are so reluctant to accept any criticism.

Secondly, we can observe another transformation in the

---

57. Cf. Demosthenes, *Orations:* 4,51; 6,31; 9,3; 58,68; Fr. 21.

problematization of *parrhesia: parrhesia* is increasingly linked to another kind of political institution, viz., *monarchy.* Freedom of speech must now be used towards the king. But obviously, in such a monarchic situation, *parrhesia* is much more dependent upon the personal qualities both of the king (who must choose to accept or reject the use of *parrhesia),* and of the king's advisors. *Parrhesia* is no longer an institutional right or privilege—as in a democratic city—but is much more a personal attitude, a choice of *bios.*

This transformation is evident, for example, in Aristotle. The word *parrhesia* is rarely used by Aristotle, but it does occur in four or five places.[58] There is, however, no political analysis of the concept of *parrhesia* as connected with any political institution. For when the word occurs, it is always either in relation to monarchy, or as a personal feature of the ethical, moral character.

In the *Constitution of Athens,* Aristotle gives an example of positive, critical *parrhesia* in the tyrannic administration of Pisistratus. As you know, Aristotle considered Pisistratus to be a humane and beneficent tyrant whose reign was very fruitful for Athens. And Aristotle gives the following account of how Pisistratus met a small landowner after he had imposed a ten percent tax on all produce:

> ... [Pisistratus] often made expeditions in person into the country to inspect it and to settle disputes between individuals, that they might not come into the city and neglect their farms. It was in one of the progresses that, as the story goes, Pisistratus had his adventure with the man

---

58. Cf. Aristotle, *Eth. Nic.* 1124b29, 1165a29; *Pol.* 1313b15; *Rhet.* 1382b20; *Rhet. Al.* 1432b18.

of Hymettus, who was cultivating the spot afterwards known as "Tax-free Farm." He saw a man digging and working at a very stony piece of ground, and being surprised he sent his attendant to ask what he got out of this plot of land. "Aches and pains," said the man; "and that's what Pisistratus ought to have his tenth of." The man spoke without knowing who his questioner was; but Pisistratus was so pleased with his frank speech [*parrhesia*] and his industry that he granted him exemption.[59]

So *parrhesia* occurs here in the monarchic situation.

The word is also used by Aristotle in the *Nicomachean Ethics* [Book IV, 1124b28], not to characterize a political practice or institution, but as a trait of the magnanimous man, the *megalopsychos* [μεγαλόψυχος]. Some of the other characteristics of the magnanimous man are more or less related to the parrhesiastic character and attitude. For example, the *megalopsychos* is courageous, but he is not one who likes danger so much that he runs out to greet it, i.e., he is not "φιλοκίνδυνος." His courage is rational [1124b7–9]. He prefers *aletheia* to *doxa*, truth to opinion. He does not like flatterers. And since he looks down on [καταφρονεῖν] other men, he is "outspoken and frank" [1124b28]. He uses *parrhesia* to speak the truth because he is able to recognize the faults of others: he is conscious of his own difference from them, of his own superiority.

So you see that for Aristotle, *parrhesia* is either a moral-ethical quality, or pertains to free speech as addressed to a monarch. Increasingly, these personal and moral features of *parrhesia* become more pronounced.

---

59. Aristotle, *Constitution of Athens*, Trans. F. G. Kenyon, 16.

4.
Parrhesia in the Care of the Self

SOCRATIC *PARRHESIA*

I would now like to analyze a new form of *parrhesia* which was emerging and developing even before Isocrates, Plato, and Aristotle. There are, of course, important similarities and analogous relationships between the political *parrhesia* we have been examining and this new form of *parrhesia*. But in spite of these similarities, a number of specific features, directly related to the figure of Socrates, characterize and differentiate this new Socratic *parrhesia*.

In selecting a testimony about Socrates as a parrhesiastic figure, I have chosen Plato's *Laches* (or "on Courage" [Περὶ ανδρείας]); and this, for several reasons. First, although this Platonic dialogue, the *Laches, is* rather short, the word *parrhesia* appears three times [178a5, 179cl, 189al]—which is rather a lot when one takes into account how infrequently Plato uses the word.

At the beginning of the dialogue it is also interesting to note that the different participants are characterized by their *parrhesia*. Lysimachus and Melesias, two of the participants, say that they will speak their minds freely, using *parrhesia* to confess that they have done or accomplished nothing very important, glorious, or special in their own lives. And they make this confession to two other older citizens, Laches and Nicias (both of them quite famous generals), in the hope that they, too, will speak openly and frankly—for they are old enough, influential enough, and glorious enough to be frank and not hide what they truly think. But this passage [178a5] is not the main one I would like to quote since it employs *parrhesia* in an everyday sense, and is not an instance of Socratic *parrhesia*.

From a strictly theoretical point of view the dialogue is a failure because no one in the dialogue is able to give a rational, true, and satisfactory definition of *courage*—which is the topic of the piece. But in spite of the fact that even Socrates himself is not able to give such a definition, at the end of the dialogue Nicias, Laches, Lysimachus, and Melesias all agree that Socrates would be the best teacher for their sons. And so Lysimachus and Melesias ask him to adopt this role. Socrates accepts, saying that everyone should try to take care of himself and of his sons [201b4]. And here you find a notion which, as some of you know, I like a lot: the concept of *"epimeleia heautou,"* the "care of the self." We have, then, I think, a movement visible throughout this dialogue from the parrhesiastic figure of Socrates to the problem of the care of the self.

Before we read the specific passages in the text that I would like to quote, however, we need to recall the situation at the beginning of the dialogue. But since the *Laches* is very complex and interwoven, I shall do so only briefly and schematically.

Two elderly men, Lysimachus and Melesias, are concerned about the kind of education they should give to their sons. Both of them belong to eminent Athenian families; Lysimachus is the son of Aristeides "the Just" and Melesias is the son of Thucydides the Elder. But although their own fathers were illustrious in their own day, Lysimachus and Melesias have accomplished nothing very special or glorious in their own lives: no important military campaigns, no significant political roles. They use *parrhesia* to admit this publicly. And they have also asked themselves the question, How is it that from such good *genos* [γένος], from such good stock, from such a noble family, they were both unable to distinguish themselves? Clearly, as their own experience shows, having a high birth and belonging to a noble Athenian house are not sufficient to endow someone with the aptitude and the ability to assume a prominent position or role in the city. They realize that something more is needed, viz., education.

But what kind of education? When we consider that the dramatic date of the *Laches* is around the end of the Fifth Century, at a time when a great many individuals—most of them presenting themselves as Sophists—claimed that they could provide young people with a good education, we can recognize here a problematic which is common to a number of Platonic dialogues. The educational techniques that were being propounded around this time often dealt with several aspects of education, e.g., rhetoric (learning how to address a jury or a political assembly), various sophistic techniques, and occasionally military education and training. In Athens at this time there was also a major problem being debated regarding the best way to educate and train the infantry soldiers, who were largely inferior to the Spartan hoplites. And all of the political, social, and institutional concerns about education, which form the general context of this dialogue, are related to the problem of *parrhesia*. In the political field we saw that there was a need for a *parrhesiastes* who could speak the truth about political institutions and decisions, and the problem there was knowing how to recognize such a truth-teller. In its basic form, this same problem now reappears in the field of education. For if you yourself are not well-educated, how then can you decide what constitutes a good education? And if people are to be educated, they must receive the truth from a competent teacher. But how can we distinguish the good, truth-telling teachers from the bad or inessential ones?

It is in order to help them come to such a decision that Lysimachus and Melesius ask Nicias and Laches to witness a performance given by Stesilaus—a man who claims to be

a teacher of *hoplomachia* [ὁπλομαχία] or the art of fighting
with heavy arms. This teacher is an athlete, technician, actor,
and artist. Which means that although he is very skillful in
handling weapons, he does not use his skill to actually fight
the enemy, but only to make money by giving public perfor-
mances and teaching the young men. The man is a kind of
sophist for the martial arts. After seeing his skills demonstrat-
ed in this public performance, however, neither Lysimachus
nor Melesius is able to decide whether this sort of skill in
fighting would constitute part of a good education. So they
turn to two well-known figures of their time, Nicias and
Laches, and ask their advice [178a–181d].

   Nicias is an experienced military general who won several victories on the battlefield, and was an important political
leader. Laches is also a respected general, although he does not
play as significant a role in Athenian politics. Both of them
give their opinions about Stesilaus' demonstration, and it
turns out that they are in complete disagreement regarding the
value of this military skill. Nicias thinks that this military
technician has done well, and that his skill may be able to provide the young with a good military education [181e–182d].
Laches disagrees, and argues that the Spartans, who are the
best soldiers in Greece, never have recourse to such teachers.
Moreover, he thinks that Stesilaus is not a soldier since he has
never won any real victories in battle [182d–184c]. Through
this disagreement we see that not only ordinary citizens without any special qualities are unable to decide what is the best
kind of education, and who is able to teach skills worth learning, but even those who have long military and political experience, like Nicias and Laches, cannot come to a unanimous
decision.

   In the end, however, Nicias and Laches both agree that

despite their fame, their important role in Athenian affairs, their age, their experience, and so on, they should refer to Socrates—who has been there all along—to see what he thinks. And after Socrates reminds them that education concerns the care of the soul [185d], Nicias explains why he will allow his soul to be "tested" by Socrates, i.e., why he will play the Socratic parrhesiastic game. And this explanation of Nicias' is, I think, a portrayal of Socrates as a *parrhesiastes:*

NICIAS: You strike me as not being aware that, whoever comes into close contact with Socrates and has any talk with him face to face, is bound to be drawn round and round by him in the course of the argument—though it may have started at first on a quite different theme—and cannot stop until he is led into giving an account of himself, of the manner in which he now spends his days, and of the kind of life he has lived hitherto; and when once he has been led into that, Socrates will never let him go until he has thoroughly and properly put all his ways to the test. Now I am accustomed to him, and so I know that one is bound to be thus treated by him, and further, that I myself shall certainly get the same treatment also. For I delight, Lysimachus, in conversing with the man, and see no harm in our being reminded of any past or present misdoing: nay, one must needs take more careful thought for the rest of one's life, if one does not fly from his words but is willing, as Solon said, and zealous to learn as long as one lives, and does not expect to get good sense by the mere arrival of old age. So to me there is nothing unusual, or unpleasant either, in being tried and tested by Socrates; in fact, I knew pretty well all the time that our argument would not be about the boys if Socrates were present, but about ourselves. Let me therefore repeat that there is no objection on my part to holding a debate with Socrates after the fashion that he likes...[60]

Nicias' speech describes the parrhesiastic game of Socrates from the point of view of the one who is "tested." But unlike the *parrhesiastes* who addresses the *demos* in the assembly, for example, here we have a parrhesiastic game which requires a personal, face to face relationship. Thus the beginning of the quote states: "whoever comes into close contact with Socrates and has any talk with him face to face..." [187e]. Socrates' interlocutor must get in touch with him, establish some *proximity* to him in order to play this parrhesiastic game. That is the first point.

Secondly, in this relationship to Socrates, the listener is led by Socrates' discourse. The passivity of the Socratic hearer, however, is not the same kind of passivity as that of a listener in the Assembly. The passivity of a listener in the political parrhesiastic game consists in being persuaded by what he listens to. Here, the listener is led by the Socratic *logos* into "giving an account"—*didonai logon* [διδόναι λόγον]"—of "himself, of the manner in which he now spends his days, and of the kind of life he has lived hitherto" [187e–188a]. Because we are inclined to read such texts through the glasses of our Christian culture, however, we might interpret this description of the Socratic game as a practice where the one who is being led by Socrates' discourse must give an autobiographical account of his life, or a confession of his faults. But such an interpretation would miss the real meaning of the text. For

---

60. Plato, *Laches*. Trans. W. R. M. Lamb, 187e–188c

when we compare this passage with similar descriptions of
Socrates' method of examination—as in the *Apology, Alcibiades
Major,* or the *Gorgias,* where we also find the idea that to be led
by the Socratic *logos* is to "give an account" of oneself—we see
very clearly that what is involved is not a confessional autobi-
ography. In Plato's or Xenophon's portrayals of him, we never
see Socrates requiring an examination of conscience or a confession of sins. Here, giving an account of your life, your *bios,*
is also not to give a narrative of the historical events that have
taken place in your life, but rather to demonstrate whether you
are able to show that there is a relation between the rational
discourse, the *logos,* you are able to use, and the way that you
live. Socrates is inquiring into the way that *logos* gives form to
a person's style of life; for he is interested in discovering
whether there is a harmonic relation between the two. Later
on in this same dialogue [190d–194b] for example, when
Socrates asks Laches to give the reason for his courage, he
wants not a narrative of Laches' exploits in the Peloponnesian
War, but for Laches to attempt to disclose the *logos* which gives
rational, intelligible form to his courage. Socrates' role, then,
is to ask for a rational accounting of a person's life.

This role is characterized in the text as that of a *"basanos"*
[βασανος] or "touchstone" which *tests* the degree of accord
between a person's life and its principle of intelligibility or
logos: "...Socrates will never let [his listener] go until he has
thoroughly and properly put all his ways to the test [πρὶν ἂν
βασανίσῃ ταῦτα εὖ τε καὶ καλῶς ἅπαντα]" [188a]. The
Greek word *basanos* refers to a "touchstone", i.e., a black stone
which is used to test the genuineness of gold by examining the
streak left on the stone when "touched" by the gold in question. Similarly, Socrates' "basanic" role enables him to determine the true nature of the relation between the *logos* and *bios*

of those who come into contact with him.[61]

Then, in the second part of this quotation, Nicias explains that as a result of Socrates' examination, one becomes willing to care for the manner in which he lives the rest of his life, wanting now to live in the best possible way; and this willingness takes the form of a zeal to learn and to educate oneself no matter what one's age.

Laches' speech, which immediately follows, describes Socrates' parrhesiastic game from the perspective of one who has inquired into Socrates' role as a touchstone. For the problem arises of knowing how we can be sure that Socrates himself is a good *basanos* for testing the relation between *logos* and *bios* in his listener's life.

> LACHES: I have but a single mind, Nicias, in regard to discussions, or if you like, a double rather than a single one. For you might think me a lover, and yet also a hater, of discussions: for when I hear a man discussing virtue or any kind of wisdom, one who is truly a man and worthy of his argument, I am exceedingly delighted; I take the speaker and his speech together, and observe how they

---

61. In the *Gorgias,* Plato writes: "SOC. If my soul were gold, Callicles, don't you think I'd delight in finding a touchstone to put that gold to the test? The best touchstone available, one which if I applied it and the stone agreed with me that my soul had been well cared for, I might be assured at last that I sufficed and needed no other test? CAL. Why ask that question, Socrates? SOC. I'll tell you. I think I've been lucky to meet a real godsend in you. CAL. Why so? SOC. Because I well know that should you agree with me in the things my soul believes, they are then the very truth. For I think that whoever is to test a soul sufficiently about correctness of life or the lack of it needs three things, of which you have: knowlege, kind regard, and frankness [παρρησία]." 486a–487a; R. E. Allen translation.

sort and harmonize with each other. Such a man is exactly what I understand by "musical"—he has tuned himself
with the fairest harmony, not that of a lyre or other enter-
taining instrument, but has made a true concord of his
own life between his words and his deeds, not in the
Ionian, no, nor in the Phrygian nor in the Lydian, but
simply in the Dorian mode, which is the sole Hellenic
harmony. Such a man makes me rejoice with his utterance, and anyone would judge me then a lover of discussion, so eagerly do I take in what he says: but a man who
shows the opposite character gives me pain, and the better he seems to speak, the more I am pained, with the
result, in this case, that I am judged a hater of discussion.
Now of Socrates' words I have no experience, but formerly, I fancy, I have made trial of his deeds; and there
I found him living up to any fine words however freely
spoken. So if he has that gift as well, his wish is mine, and
I should be very glad to be cross-examined by such a man,
and should not chafe at learning.[62]

As you can see, this speech in part answers the question of
how to determine the visible criteria, the personal qualities,
which entitle Socrates to assume the role of the *basanos*
of other people's lives. From information given at the beginning of the *Laches* we have learned that by the dramatic date
of the dialogue, Socrates is not very well known, that he is not
regarded as an eminent citizen, that he is younger than Nicias
and Laches, and that he has no special competence in the field
of military training—with this exception: he exhibited great

---

62. Plato, *Laches*. Trans. W. R. M. Lamb, 188c–189a.

courage in the battle at Delium[63] where Laches was the commanding general. Why, then, would two famous and older generals submit to Socrates' cross-examinations? Laches, who is not as interested in philosophical or political discussions, and who prefers deeds to words throughout the dialogue (in contrast to Nicias), gives the answer. For he says that there is a harmonic relation between what Socrates says and what he does, between his words *(logoi)* and his deeds *(erga)*. Thus not only is Socrates himself able to give an account of his own life, such an account is already visible in his behavior since there is not the slightest discrepancy between what he says and what he does. He is a *"mousikos aner"* [μουσικος ἀνήρ]. In Greek culture, and in most of Plato's other dialogues, the phrase *"mousikos aner"* denotes a person who is devoted to the Muses—a cultured person of the liberal arts. Here the phrase refers to someone who exhibits a kind of ontological harmony where the *logos* and *bios* of such a person is in harmonic accord. And this harmonic relation is also a Dorian harmony.

As you know, there were four kinds of Greek harmony:[64] the Lydian mode which Plato dislikes because it is too solemn; the Phrygian mode which Plato associates with the passions; the Ionian mode which is too soft and effeminate; and the Dorian mode which is courageous.

The harmony between word and deed in Socrates' life is Dorian, and was manifested in the courage he showed at Delium. This harmonic accord is what distinguishes Socrates from a sophist: the sophist can give very fine and beautiful discourses on courage, but is not courageous himself. This accord

---

63. Cf. Plato, *Symposium*, 221a–b; *Laches*, 181b, 189b.
64. Cf. Plato, *Republic*, III, 398c–399e; Aristotle, *Politics*, VIII, 7.

is also why Laches can say of Socrates: "I found him living up to any fine words however freely spoken [λόγον καὶ πάσης παρρησίας]." Socrates is able to use rational, ethically valuable, fine, and beautiful discourse; but unlike the sophist, he can use *parrhesia* and speak freely because what he says accords exactly with what he thinks, and what he thinks accords exactly with what he does. And so Socrates—who is truly free and courageous—can therefore function as a parrhesiastic figure.

Just as was the case in the political field, the parrhesiastic figure of Socrates also discloses the truth in speaking, is courageous in his life and in his speech, and confronts his listener's opinion in a critical manner. But Socratic *parrhesia* differs from political *parrhesia* in a number of ways. It appears in a personal relationship between two human beings, and not in the *parrhesiastes'* relation to the *demos* or the king. And in addition to the relationships we noticed between *logos*, truth, and courage in political *parrhesia*, with Socrates a new element now emerges, viz., *bios*. *Bios* is the focus of Socratic *parrhesia*. On Socrates' or the philosopher's side, the *bios-logos* relation is a Dorian harmony which grounds Socrates' parrhesiastic role, and which, at the same time, constitutes the visible criterion for his function as the *basanos* or touchstone. On the interlocutor's side, the *bios-logos* relation is disclosed when the interlocutor gives an account of his life, and its harmony tested by contact with Socrates. Since he possesses in his relation to truth all the qualities that need to be disclosed in the interlocutor, Socrates can test the relation to truth of the interlocutor's existence. The aim of this Socratic parrhesiastic activity, then, is to lead the interlocutor to the choice of that kind of life *(bios)* that will be in Dorian-harmonic accord with *logos*, virtue, courage, and truth.

In Euripides' *Ion* we saw the problematization of *parrhesia* in the form of a game between *logos,* truth, and *genos* (birth) in the relations between the gods and mortals; and Ion's parrhesiastic role was grounded in a mythical genealogy descended from Athens: *parrhesia* was the civic right of the well-born citizen of Athens. In the realm of political institutions the problematization of *parrhesia* involved a game between *logos,* truth, and *nomos* (law); and the *parrhesiastes* was needed to disclose those truths which would ensure the salvation or welfare of the city. *Parrhesia* here was the personal quality of a courageous orator and political leader, or the personal quality of an advisor to the king. And now with Socrates the problematization of *parrhesia* takes the form of a game between *logos,* truth, and *bios* (life) in the realm of a personal teaching relation between two human beings. And the truth that the parrhesiastic discourse discloses is the truth of someone's life, i.e., the kind of relation someone has to truth: how he constitutes himself as someone who has to know the truth through *mathesis,* and how this relation to truth is ontologically and ethically manifest in his own life. *Parrhesia,* in turn, becomes an ontological characteristic of the *basanos,* whose harmonic relation to truth can function as a touchstone. The objective of the cross-examinations Socrates conducts in his role of the touchstone, then, is to test the specific relation to truth of the other's existence.

In Euripides' *Ion, parrhesia* was opposed to Apollo's silence; in the political sphere *parrhesia* was opposed to the *demos'* will, or to those who flatter the desires of the majority or the monarch. In this third, Socratic-philosophical game, *parrhesia* is opposed to self-ignorance and the false teachings of the sophists.

Socrates' role as a *basanos* appears very clearly in the *Laches;* but in other Platonic texts—the *Apology,* for example—this role is presented as a mission assigned to Socrates by the oracular deity at Delphi,[65] viz., Apollo—the same god who kept silent in *Ion*. And just as Apollo's oracle was open to all who wished to consult it, so Socrates offered himself up to anyone as a questioner.[66] The Delphic oracle was also so enigmatic and obscure that one could not understand it without knowing what sort of question one was asking, and what kind of meaning the oracular pronouncement could take in one's life. Similarly, Socrates' discourse requires that one overcome self-ignorance about one's own situation. But, of course, there are major differences. For example, the oracle foretold what would happen to you, whereas Socratic *parrhesia* means to disclose who you are—not your relation to future events, but your present relation to truth.

I do not mean to imply that there is any strict chronological progression among the various forms of *parrhesia* we have noted. Euripides died in 407 B.C. and Socrates was put to death in 399 B.C. In ancient culture the continuation of ideas and themes is also more pronounced. And we are also quite limited in the number of documents available from this period. So there is no precise chronology. The forms of *parrhesia* we see in Euripides did not generate a very long tradition. And as the Hellenistic monarchies grew and developed, political *parrhesia* increasingly assumed the form of a personal relation between the monarch and his advisors, thereby coming closer to the Socratic form. Increased emphasis was placed on the royal art of statesmanship and the moral education of the king. And the Socratic type of *parrhesia* had a long tradition through the Cynics and other Socratic Schools. So the divisions are almost contemporary when they appear, but the historical

---

65. Cf. Plato, *Apology*, 21a–23b, 33c.
66. *Ibid.*, 33b.

destinies of the three are not the same.

In Plato, and in what we know of Socrates through Plato, a major problem concerns the attempt to determine how to bring the political *parrhesia* involving *logos*, truth, and *nomos* so that it coincides with the ethical *parrhesia* involving *logos*, truth, and *bios*. How can philosophical truth and moral virtue relate to the city through the *nomos?* You see this issue in the *Apology*, the *Crito*, the *Republic*, and in the *Laws*. There is a very interesting text in the *Laws*, for example, where Plato says that even in the city ruled by good laws there is still a need for someone who will use *parrhesia* to tell the citizens what moral conduct they must observe.[67] Plato distinguishes between the Guardians of the Laws and the *parrhesiastes*, who does not monitor the application of the laws, but, like Socrates, speaks the truth about the good of the city, and gives advice from an ethical, philosophical standpoint. And, as far as I know, it is the only text in Plato where the one who uses *parrhesia* is a kind of political figure in the field of the law.

In the Cynic tradition, which also derives from Socrates, the problematic relation between *nomos* and *bios* will become a direct opposition. For in this tradition, the Cynic philosopher is regarded as the only one capable of assuming the role of the

---

67. Plato writes: "…there are other matters which make no small difference, about which it is difficult to be persuasive, and which are in fact the task of the god, if it were somehow possible to get the orders themselves from him; as things stand now, what is required, in all probability, is some daring human being, who by giving unusual honor to outspokenness [*parrhesia*] will say what in his opinion is best for the city and the citizens. Speaking before an audience of corrupt souls, he will order what is fitting and becoming to the whole political regime; opposing the greatest desires, and having no human ally, all alone will he follow reason alone." [*The Laws.* Trans. Thomas L. Pangle, Book VIII, 835c]

parrhesiastes. And, as we shall see in the case of Diogenes, he must adopt a permanent negative and critical attitude towards any kind of political institution, and towards any kind of *nomos*.

The last time we met we analyzed some texts from Plato's *Laches* where we saw the emergence, with Socrates, of a new "philosophical" *parrhesia* very different from the previous forms we examined.[68] In the *Laches* we had a game with five main players. Two of them, Lysimachus and Melesius, were well-born Athenian citizens from noble houses who were unable to assume a parrhesiastic role—for they did not know how to educate their own children. So they turned to a general and a political statesman, Laches and Nicias, who were also unable to play the role of *parrhesiastes*. Laches and Nicias, in turn, were obliged to appeal for help to Socrates, who appears as the real parrhesiastic figure. We see in these transitional moves a successive displacement of the parrhesiastic role from the well-born Athenian and the political leader—who formerly possessed the role—to the philosopher, Socrates. Taking the *Laches* as our point of departure, we can now observe in Greco-Roman culture the rise and development of this new kind of *parrhesia* which, I think, can be characterized as follows.

First, this *parrhesia* is philosophical, and has been put into practice for centuries by the philosophers. Indeed, a large part of the philosophical activity that transpired in Greco-Roman culture required playing certain parrhesiastic games. Very schematically, I think that this philosophical role involved three types of parrhesiastic activity, all of them related to one

---

68. Fifth Lecture: 21 November 1983.

another. (1) Insofar as the philosopher had to discover and to teach certain truths about the world, nature, etc., he assumed an epistemic role. (2) Taking a stand towards the city, the laws, political institutions, and so on, required, in addition, a political role. (3) And parrhesiastic activity also endeavored to elaborate the nature of the relationships between truth and one's style of life, or truth and an ethics and aesthetics of the self. *Parrhesia* as it appears in the field of philosophical activity in Greco-Roman culture is not primarily a concept or theme, but a *practice* which tries to shape the specific relations individuals have to themselves. And I think that our own moral subjectivity is rooted, at least in part, in these practices. More precisely, I think that the decisive criterion which identifies the *parrhesiastes* is not to be found in his birth, nor in his citizenship, nor in his intellectual competence, but in the harmony which exists between his *logos* and his *bios*.

Secondly, the target of this new *parrhesia* is not to persuade the Assembly, but to convince someone that he must take care of himself and of others; and this means that he must *change his life*. This theme of changing one's life, of conversion, becomes very important from the Fourth Century B.C. to the beginnings of Christianity. It is essential to philosophical parrhesiastic practices. Of course conversion is not completely different from the change of mind that an orator, using his *parrhesia*, wished to bring about when he asked his fellow citizens to wake up, to refuse what they previously accepted, or to accept what they previously refused. But in philosophical practice the notion of changing one's mind takes on a more general and expanded meaning since it is no longer just a matter of altering one's belief or opinion, but of changing one's style of life, one's relation to others, and one's relation to oneself.

Thirdly, these new parrhesiastic practices imply a complex set of connections between the self and truth. For not only are these practices supposed to endow the individual with self-knowledge, this self-knowledge in turn is supposed to grant access to truth and further knowledge. The circle implied in knowing the truth about oneself in order to know the truth is characteristic of parrhesiastic practice since the Fourth Century, and has been one of the problematic enigmas of Western Thought—e.g., as in Descartes or Kant.

And a final point I would like to underscore about this philosophical *parrhesia* is that it has recourse to numerous techniques quite different from the techniques of persuasive discourse previously utilized; and it is no longer specifically linked to the *agora,* or to the king's court, but can now be utilized in numerous diverse places.

THE PRACTICE OF *PARRHESIA*

In this session and next week—in the last seminar meeting— I would like to analyze philosophical *parrhesia* from the standpoint of its practices. By the "practice" of *parrhesia* I mean two things: First, the use of *parrhesia* in specific types of human relationships (which I shall address this evening); and secondly, the procedures and techniques employed in such relationships (which will be the topic of our last session).

In Human Relationships

Because of the lack of time, and to assist in the clarity of the presentation, I would like to distinguish three kinds of human relationships which are implied in the use of this new philosophical *parrhesia*. But, of course, this is only a general schema, for there are several intermediate forms.

First, *parrhesia* occurs as an activity in the framework of small groups of people, or in the context of community life. Secondly, *parrhesia* can be seen in human relationships occuring in the framework of public life. And finally, *parrhesia* occurs in the context of individual personal relationships. More specifically, we can say that *parrhesia* as a feature of community life was highly regarded by the Epicureans; *parrhesia* as a public activity or public demonstration was a significant aspect of Cynicism, as well as that type of philosophy that was a mixture of Cynicism and Stoicism; and *parrhesia* as an aspect of personal relationships is found more frequently either in Stoicism or in a generalized or common Stoicism characteristic of such writers as Plutarch.

Community life

Although the Epicureans, with the importance they gave to friendship, emphasized community life more than other philosophers at this time, nonetheless one can also find some Stoic groups, as well as Stoic or Stoico-Cynic philosophers, who acted as moral and political advisors to various circles and aristocratic clubs. For example, Musonius Rufus was spiritual advisor to Nero's cousin, Rubellius Plautus, and his circle; and the Stoico-Cynic philosopher Demetrius was advisor to a liberal anti-aristocratic group around Thrasea Paetus.[69] Thrasea Paetus, a Roman senator, committed suicide after being condemned to death by the senate during Nero's reign. And Demetrius was the *régisseur,* *I* would say, of his suicide.

---

69. Cf. Michel Foucault, *Le Souci de soi,* 67–68; Cora E. Lutz, *Musonius Rufus,* 14ff.

So besides the community life of the Epicureans there are other intermediate forms. There is also the very interesting case of Epictetus. Epictetus was a Stoic for whom the practice of speaking openly and frankly was also very important. He directed a school about which we know a few things from the four surviving volumes of Epictetus' *Discourses* as recorded by Arrian. We know, for example, that Epictetus' school was located at Nicopolis in a permanent structure which enabled students to share in a real community life.[70] Public lectures and teaching sessions were given where the public was invited, and where individuals could ask questions—although sometimes such individuals were mocked and twitted by the masters. We also know that Epictetus conducted both public conversations with his disciples in front of a class, and private consultations and interviews. His school was a kind of *école normale* for those who wanted to become philosophers or moral advisors.

So when I tell you that philosophical *parrhesia* occurs as an activity in three types of relationship, it must be clear that the forms I have chosen are only guiding examples; the actual practices were, of course, much more complicated and interrelated.

First, then, the example of the Epicurean groups regarding the practice of *parrhesia* in community life. Unfortunately, we know very few things about the Epicurean communities, and even less about the parrhesiastic practices in these communities—which explains the brevity of my exposition. But we do have a text entitled "Περὶ παρρησίας" [*On Frank Speaking*] written by Philodemus (who is recording the lec-

---

70. Cf. B. L. Hijmans, *Askesis: Notes on Epictetus' Educational System.*

tures [σχολαί] of Zeno of Sidon).[71] The text is not complete in
its entirety, but the existing manuscript pieces come from the
ruins of the Epicurean library discovered at Herculaneum
near the end of the Nineteenth Century. What has been preserved is very fragmentary and rather obscure; and I must confess that without some commentary from the Italian scholar,
Marcello Gigante, I would not have understood much of this
fragmentary Greek text.[72]

I would like to underline the following points from this
treatise.

First, Philodemus regards *parrhesia* not only as a quality,
virtue, or personal attitude, but also as a *techne* comparable
both to the art of medicine and to the art of piloting a boat.[73]
As you know, the comparison between medicine and navigation is a very traditional one in Greek culture. But even without this reference to *parrhesia*, the comparison of medicine and
navigation is interesting for the following two reasons.

(1) The reason why the pilot's *techne* of navigation is similar to the physician's *techne* of medicine is that in both cases,
the necessary theoretical knowledge required also demands
practical training in order to be useful. Furthermore, in order
to put these techniques to work, one has to take into account
not only the general rules and principles of the art, but also
particular data which are always specific to a given situation.

------

71. Philodemus, Περὶ παρρησίας. Ed. A. Olivieri, 1914.
72. Cf. Marcello Gigante, "Philodème: Sur la liberté de parole"; "Motivi
paideutici nell' opera filodemea sulla libertà di parola"; and "'Philosophia
Medicans' in Filodemo."
73. Gigante writes: "Les caractéristiques qui distinguent les *technai* στοχ-
αστικαί comme la médecine et l'art du nautonier chez Aristote sont les
mêmes que celles qui, chez Zénon-Philodème, définissent la *parrhesia*"
["Philodème: Sur la liberté de parole," 206].

One must take into account the particular circumstances, and
also what the Greeks called the *kairos* [καιρός], or "the critical
moment."[74] The concept of the *kairos*—*the* decisive or crucial
moment or opportunity—has always had a significant role in
Greek thought for epistemological, moral, and technical reasons.[75] What is of interest here is that since Philodemus is now
associating *parrhesia* with piloting and medicine, it is also
being regarded as a technique which deals with individual
cases, specific situations, and the choice of the *kairos* or decisive moment.[76] Utilizing our modern vocabulary, we can say
that navigation, medicine, and the practice of *parrhesia* are all
"clinical techniques."

(2) Another reason why the Greeks often associated medicine and navigation is that in the case of both techniques, one
person (the pilot or physician) must make the decisions, give
orders and instructions, exercise power and authority, while
the others—the crew, the patient, the staff—must obey if the
desired end is to be achieved. Hence navigation and medicine
are also both related to politics. For in politics the choice of
the opportunity, the best moment, is also crucial; and someone

---

74. In the *Nicomachaen Ethics* Aristotle writes: "…matters concerned with
conduct and questions of what is good for us have no fixity, any more than
matters of health. The general account being of this nature, the account of
particular cases is yet more lacking in exactness; for they do not fall under
any art or set of precepts, but the agents themselves must in each case consider what is appropriate to the occasion [πρὸς τὸν καιρὸν], as happens
also in the art of medicine or of navigation." [Trans. W. D. Ross, 1104a4–9]
75. Cf. Michel Foucault, *L'Usage des plaisirs*, 68–70.
76. Fragment 226 of Democritus also associates *parrhesia* with *kairos*:
"οἰκήϊον ἐλευθερίης παρρησίη, κίνδυνος δὲ ἡ τοῦ καιροῦ διάγνωσις"
["Freedom of speech is the sign of freedom; but the danger lies in discern-
ing the right occasion"—K. Freeman translation]. Cf. Hermann Diels, *Die
Fragmente der Vorsokratiker,* Vol. 1, 190.

is also supposed to be more competent than the others—and therefore has the right to give the orders that the others must obey.[77] In politics, then, there are indispensible techniques which lie at the root of statesmanship considered as the art of governing people.

If I mention this ancient affinity between medicine, navigation, and politics, it is in order to indicate that with the addition of the parrhesiastic techniques of "spiritual guidance," a corpus of interrelated clinical *technai* was constituted during the Hellenistic period. Of course, the *techne* of piloting or navigation is primarily of metaphorical significance. But an analysis of the various relations which Greco-Roman culture believed existed between the three clinical activities of medicine, politics, and the practice of *parrhesia* would be important.

Several centuries later, Gregory of Nazianzus [c. A.D. 329–389] would call spiritual guidance the "technique of techniques"—*"ars artium," "techne technon"* [τέχνη τέχνων]. This expression is significant since statesmanship or political *techne* was previously regarded as the *techne technon* or the Royal Art. But from the Fourth Century A.D. to the Seventeenth Century in Europe, the expression *"techne technon"* usually refers to spiritual guidance as the most significant clinical technique. This characterization of *parrhesia* as a *techne* in relation to medicine, piloting, and politics is indicative of the transformation of *parrhesia* into a philosophical practice. From the physician's art of governing patients and the king's art of governing the city and its subjects, we move to the philosopher's art of governing himself and acting as a kind of "spiritual guide" for other people.

---

77. Cf. Aristotle, *Politics*, 1324b29.

Another aspect of Philodemus' text concerns the references it contains about the structure of the Epicurean communities; but commentators on Philodemus disagree about the exact form, complexity, and hierarchical organization of such communities. DeWitt thinks that the existing hierarchy was very well-established and complex; whereas Gigante thinks that it was much simpler.[78] It seems that there were at least two categories of teachers and two types of teaching in the Epicurean schools and groups.

There was "classroom" teaching where a teacher addressed a group of students; and there was also instruction in the form of personal interviews where a teacher would give advice and precepts to individual community members. Whereas the lower-ranked teachers only taught classes, the higher-level teachers both taught classes and gave personal interviews. Thus a distinction was drawn between general teaching and personal instruction or guidance. This distinction is not a difference in content, as between theoretical and practical subject matters—especially since studies in physics, cosmology, and natural law had ethical significance for the Epicureans. Nor is it a difference in instruction contrasting ethical theory with its practical application. Rather the difference marks a distinction in the pedagogical relationship between teacher and disciple or student. In the Socratic situation, there was one procedure which enabled the interlocutor to discover the truth about himself, the relation of his *bios* to *logos;* and this same procedure, at the same time,

---

78. Cf. Norman DeWitt, "Organization and Procedure in Epicurean Groups," "Epicurean *Contubernium,*" and *Epicurus and His Philosophy* [Chapter V: The New School in Athens]; Marcello Gigante, "Filodemo sulla libertà di parola," and "Motivi paideutici nell' opera filodemea sulla libertà di parola."

also enabled him to gain access to additional truths (about the world, ideas, the nature of the soul, and so on). With the Epicurean schools, however, there is the pedagogical relation of guidance where the master helps the disciple to discover the truth about himself; but there is now, in addition, a form of "authoritarian" teaching in a collective relation where someone speaks the truth to a group of others. These two types of teaching became a permanent feature of Western culture. And in the Epicurean schools we know that it was the role of the "spiritual guide" for others that was more highly valued that that of group lecturer.

I do not wish to conclude the discussion of Philodemus' text without mentioning a practice which they engaged in—what we might call "mutual confession" in a group. Some of the fragments indicate that there were group sessions or meetings where each of the community members in turn would disclose their thoughts, faults, misbehavior, and so on. We know very little about such meetings, but referring to this practice Philodemus uses an interesting expression. He speaks of this practice as "the salvation by one another"—"*to di' allelon sozesthai*" [το δι' ἀλλήλων σῷζεσθαι].[79] The word *sozesthai*—to save oneself—in the Epicurean tradition means to gain access to a good, beautiful, and happy life. It does not refer to any kind of afterlife or divine judgment. In one's own salvation, other members of the Epicurean community [The Garden] have a decisive role to play as necessary agents enabling one to discover the truth about oneself, and in helping one to gain access to a happy life. Hence the very impor-

---

79. Philodemus, Περὶ παρρησίας, Fragment 36, 17; cf. Foucault, *Le Souci de soi*, 67.

tant emphasis on friendship in the Epicurean groups.

Public life

Now I would like to move on to the practice of *parrhesia* in public life through the example of the Cynic philosophers. In the case of the Epicurean communities, we know very little about their style of life but have some idea of their doctrine as it is expressed in various texts. With the Cynics the situation is exactly reversed; for we know very little about Cynic doctrine—even if there ever was such an explicit doctrine. But we do possess numerous testimonies regarding the Cynic way of life. And there is nothing surprising about this state of affairs; for even though Cynic philosophers wrote books just like other philosophers, they were far more interested in choosing and practicing a certain way of life.

A historical problem concerning the origin of Cynicism is this. Most of the Cynics from the First Century B.C. and thereafter refer to either Diogenes or Antisthenes as the founder of the Cynic philosophy; and through these founders of Cynicism they relate themselves back to the teachings of Socrates.[80] According to Farrand Sayre,[81] however, the Cynic Sect appeared only in the Second Century B.C., or two centuries after Socrates' death. We might be a bit skeptical about a traditional explanation given for the rise of the Cynic Sects—an explanation which has been given so often to account for so many other phenomena—but it is that Cynicism is a negative form of aggressive individualism which arose with the collapse of the political structures of the ancient

---

80. Cf. Diogenes Laertius, VI, 2.
81. Cf. Farrand Sayre, *Diogenes of Sinope, A Study of Greek Cynicism.*

world. A more interesting account is given by Sayre, who explains the appearance of the Cynics on the Greek philosophical scene as a consequence of expanding conquests of the Macedonian Empire. More specifically, he notes that with Alexander's conquests various Indian philosophies—especially the monastic and ascetic teachings of Indian Sects like the Gymnosophists—became more familiar to the Greeks.

Regardless of what we can determine about the origins of Cynicism, it is a fact that the Cynics were very numerous and influential from the end of the First Century B.C. to the Fourth Century A.D. Thus in A.D. 165 Lucian, who did not like the Cynics, writes: "The city swarms with these vermin, particularly those who profess the tenets of Diogenes, Antisthenes, and Crates."[82] It seems, in fact, that the self-styled "Cynics" were so numerous that Emperor Julian, in his attempt to revive classical Greek culture, wrote a lampoon against them scorning their ignorance, their coarseness, and portraying them as a danger for the Empire and for Greco-Roman culture.[83] One of the reasons why Julian treated the Cynics so harshly was their general resemblance to the early Christians. And some of the similarities may have been more than mere superficial resemblance. For example, Peregrinus (a well known Cynic at the end of the Second Century A.D.) was considered a kind of saint by his Cynic followers, especially by those who regarded his death as a heroic emulation of the death of Heracles [Hercules]. To display his Cynic indifference [ἀδιάφορία] to death, Peregrinus committed suicide by cremating himself immediately following the Olympic Games of A.D. 167. Lucian, who witnessed the event, gives a satirical,

---

82. Lucian, "The Runaways," Trans. A. M. Harmon, 116.
83. Cf. Julian, "To the Uneducated Cynics."

derisive account.[84] Julian was also disappointed that the Cynics were not able to represent ancient Greco-Roman culture, for he hoped that there would be something like a popular philosophical movement which would compete with Christianity.

The high value which the Cynics attributed to a person's way of life does not mean that they had no interest in theoretical philosophy, but reflects their view that the manner in which a person lived was a touchstone of his relation to truth—as we saw was also the case in the Socratic tradition. The conclusion they drew from this Socratic idea, however, was that in order to proclaim the truths they accepted in a manner that would be accessible to everyone, they thought that their teachings had to consist in a very public, visible, spectacular, provocative, and sometimes scandalous way of life. The Cynics thus taught by way of examples and the explanations associated with them. They wanted their own lives to be a *blazon* of essential truths which would then serve as a guideline, or as an example for others to follow. But there is nothing in this Cynic emphasis on philosophy as an art of life which is alien to Greek philosophy. So even if we accept Sayre's hypothesis about the Indian philosophical influence on Cynic doctrine and practice, we must still recognize that the Cynic attitude is, in its basic form, just an extremely radical version of the very Greek conception of the relationship between one's way of life and knowledge of the truth. The Cynic idea that a person is nothing else but his relation to truth, and that this relation to truth takes shape or is given form in his own life—that is completely Greek.

---

84. Cf. Lucian, "The Passing of Peregrinus."

In the Platonic, Aristotelian, and Stoic traditions, philosophers referred mainly to a doctrine, text, or at least to some theoretical principles for their philosophy. In the Epicurean tradition, the followers of Epicurus refer both to a doctrine and also to the personal example set by Epicurus, whom every Epicurean tried to imitate. Epicurus originated the doctrine and was also a personification of it. But now in the Cynic tradition, the main references for the philosophy are not to the texts or doctrines, but to exemplary lives. Personal examples were also important in other philosophical schools, but in the Cynic movement—where there were no established texts, no settled, recognizable doctrine—reference was always made to certain real or mythical personalities who were taken to be the sources of Cynicism as a mode of life. Such personalities were the starting point for Cynic reflection and commentary. The mythical characters referred to included Heracles [Hercules], Odysseus [Ulysses], and Diogenes. Diogenes was an actual, historical figure, but his life became so legendary that he developed into a kind of myth as anecdotes, scandals, etc., were added to his historical life. About his actual life we do not know all that much, but it is clear that he became a kind of philosophical hero. Plato, Aristotle, Zeno of Citium, et al., were philosophical authors and authorities, for example; but they were not considered heroes. Epicurus was both a philosophical author and treated by his followers as a kind of hero. But Diogenes was primarily a heroic figure. The idea that a philosopher's life should be exemplary and heroic is important in understanding the relationship of Cynicism to Christianity, as well as for understanding Cynic *parrhesia* as a public activity.

This brings us to Cynic *parrhesia*.[85] The three main types of parrhesiastic practice utilized by the Cynics were: (1) critical preaching; (2) scandalous behavior; and (3) what I shall call the "provocative dialogue."

First, the critical preaching of the Cynics. Preaching is a form of continuous discourse. And, as you know, most of the early philosophers—especially the Stoics—would occasionally deliver speeches where they presented their doctrines. Usually, however, they would lecture in front of a rather small audience. The Cynics, in contrast, disliked this kind of elitist exclusion and preferred to address a large crowd. For example, they liked to speak in a theater, or at a place where people had gathered for a feast, religious event, athletic contest, etc. They would sometimes stand up in the middle of a theater audience and deliver a speech. This public preaching was not their own innovation, for we have testimonies of similar practices as early as the Fifth Century B.C. Some of the Sophists we see in the Platonic dialogues, for example, also engage in preaching to some extent. Cynic preaching, however, had its own specific characteristics, and is historically significant since it enabled philosophical themes about one's way of life to become popular, i.e., to come to the attention of people who stood outside the philosophical elect. From this perspective, Cynic preaching about freedom, the renunciation of luxury, Cynic criticisms of political institutions and existing moral codes, and so on, also opened the way for some Christian themes. But Christian proselytes not only spoke about themes which were often similar to the Cynics; they also took over the practice of preaching.

---

85. Cf. Giuseppe Scarpat, *Parrhesia*, 62–69 [*La parrhesia cinica*].

Preaching is still one of the main forms of truth-telling practiced in our society, and it involves the idea that the truth must be told and taught not only to the best members of the society, or to an exclusive group, but to everyone.

There is, however, very little positive doctrine in Cynic preaching: no direct affirmation of the good or bad. Instead, the Cynics refer to freedom *(eleutheria)* and self-sufficiency *(autarkeia)* as the basic criteria by which to assess any kind of behavior or mode of life. For the Cynics, the main condition for human happiness is *autarkeia*, self-sufficiency or independence, where what you need to have or what you decide to do is dependent on nothing other than you yourself. As a consequence—since the Cynics had the most radical of attitudes— they preferred a completely natural life-style. A natural life was supposed to eliminate all of the dependencies introduced by culture, society, civilization, opinion, and so on. Consequently, most of their preaching seems to have been directed against social institutions, the arbitrariness of rules of law, and any sort of life-style that was dependent upon such institutions or laws. In short, their preaching was against all social institutions insofar as such institutions hindered one's freedom and independence.

Cynic *parrhesia* also had recourse to scandalous behavior or attitudes which called into question collective habits, opinions, standards of decency, institutional rules, and so on. Several procedures were used. One of them was the inversion of roles, as can be seen from Dio Chrysostom's Fourth Discourse where the famous encounter between Diogenes and Alexander is depicted. This encounter, which was often referred to by the Cynics, does not take place in the privacy of Alexander's court but in the street, in the open. The king stands up while Diogenes sits back in his barrel. Diogenes orders Alexander to step out of his light so that he can bask in the sun. Ordering Alexander to step aside so that the sun's light can reach Diogenes is an affirmation of the direct and natural relation the philosopher has to the sun, in contrast to the mythical genealogy whereby the king, as descended from a god, was supposed to personify the sun.

The Cynics also employed the technique of displacing or transposing a rule from a domain where the rule was accepted to a domain where it was not in order to show how arbitrary the rule was. Once, during the athletic contests and horse-races of the Isthmian festival, Diogenes—who was bothering everyone with his frank remarks—took a crown of pine and put it on his head as if he had been victorious in an athletic competition. And the magistrates were very happy about this gesture because they thought it was, at last, a good occasion to punish him, to exclude him, to get rid of him. But he explained that he placed a crown upon his head because he had won a much more difficult victory against poverty, exile, desire, and his own vices than athletes who were victorious in wrestling, running, and hurling a discus.[86] And later on during the games, he saw two horses fighting and kicking each other until one of them ran off. So Diogenes went up and put a crown on the head of the horse who stood its ground.[87] These two symmetrical displacements have the effect of raising the question: What are you really doing when you award someone with a crown in the Isthmian games? For if the crown is awarded to someone as a moral victory, then Diogenes deserves a crown. But if it is only a question of superior physical

---

86. Cf. Dio Chrystosom, "The Ninth or Isthmian Discourse," 10–13.
87. *Ibid.*, 22.

strength, then there is no reason why the horse should not be given a crown.

Cynic *parrhesia* in its scandalous aspects also utilized the practice of bringing together two rules of behavior which seem contradictory and remote from one another. For example, regarding the problem of bodily needs. You eat. There is no scandal in eating, so you can eat in public (although, for the Greeks, this is not obvious and Diogenes was sometimes reproached for eating in the *agora*). Since Diogenes ate in the *agora*, he thought that there was no reason why he should not also masturbate in the *agora*; for in both cases he was satisfying a bodily need (adding that "he wished it were as easy to banish hunger by rubbing the belly").[88] Well, I will not try to conceal the shamelessness *(anaideia)* of the Cynics as a scandalous practice or technique.

As you may know, the word "cynic" comes from the Greek word meaning "dog-like" *(kynikoi);* and Diogenes was called "The Dog." In fact, the first and only contemporary reference to Diogenes is found in Aristotle's *Rhetoric*,[89] where Aristotle does not even mention the name Diogenes but just calls him "The Dog." The noble philosophers of Greece, who usually comprised an elite group, almost always disregarded the Cynics.

The Cynics also used another parrhesiastic technique, viz., the "provocative dialogue." To give you a more precise example of this type of dialogue—which derives from Socratic *parrhesia*—I have chosen a passage from the Fourth Discourse

---

88. Cf. Diogenes Laertius, VI, 46, 69; Plutarch, "Stoic Self-Contradictions," 1044b.
89. Aristotle, *Rhetoric* [3, 10, 1411a24]: "The Dog called taverns 'the mess-rooms of Attica.'"

on Kingship of Dio Chrysostom of Prusa [c.A.D.40–110].

Do you all know who Dio Chrysostom is? Well, he is a very interesting guy from the last half of the First Century and the beginning of the Second Century of our era. He was born at Prusa in Asia Minor of a wealthy Roman family who played a prominent role in the city-life. Dio's family was typical of the affluent provincial notables that produced so many writers, officers, generals, sometimes even emperors, for the Roman Empire. He came to Rome possibly as a professional rhetorician, but there are some disputes about this. An American scholar, C.P. Jones, has written a very interesting book about Dio Chrysostom which depicts the social life of an intellectual in the Roman Empire of Dio's time.[90] In Rome Dio Chrysostom became acquainted with Musonius Rufus, the Stoic philosopher, and possibly through him he became involved with some liberal circles generally opposed to personal tyrannic power. He was subsequently exiled by Domitian, who disliked his views, and thus he began a wandering life where he adopted the costume and the attitudes of the Cynics for several years. When he was finally authorized to return to Rome following Domitian's assassination, he started a new career. His former fortune was returned to him, and he became a wealthy and famous teacher. For a while, however, he had the life-style, the attitude, the habits, and the philosophical views of a Cynic philosopher. But we must keep in mind the fact that Dio Chrysostom was not a "pure" cynic; and perhaps with his intellectual background his depiction of the Cynic parrhesiastic game puts it closer to the Socratic tradition than most of the actual Cynic practices.

---

90. Cf. Christopher P. Jones, *The Roman World of Dio Chrysostom.*

In the Fourth Discourse of Dio Chrysostom I think you can find all three forms of Cynic *parrhesia*. The end of the Discourse is a kind of preaching, and throughout there are references to Diogenes' scandalous behavior and examples illustrating the provocative dialogue of Diogenes with Alexander. The topic of the Discourse is the famous encounter between Diogenes and Alexander the Great which actually took place at Corinth. The Discourse begins with Dio's thoughts concerning this meeting [1–14]; then a fictional dialogue follows portraying the nature of Diogenes' and Alexander's conversation [15–81]; and the Discourse ends with a long, continuous discussion—fictionally narrated by Diogenes—regarding three types of faulty and self-deluding styles of life [82–139].

At the very beginning of the Discourse, Dio criticizes those who present the meeting of Diogenes and Alexander as an encounter between equals: one man famous for his leadership and military victories, the other famous for his free and self-sufficient life-style and his austere and naturalistic moral virtue. Dio does not want people to praise Alexander just because he, as a powerful king, did not disregard a poor guy like Diogenes. He insists that Alexander actually felt *inferior* to Diogenes, and was also a bit envious of his reputation; for unlike Alexander, who wanted to conquer the world, Diogenes did not need anything to do what he wanted to do:

> [Alexander] himself needed his Macedonian phalanx, his Thessalian cavalry, Thracians, Paeonians, and many others if he was to go where he wished and get what he desired; but Diogenes went forth unattended in perfect safety by night as well as by day wherever he cared to go. Again, he himself required huge sums of gold and silver to carry out any of his projects; and what is more, if he

expected to keep the Macedonians and the other Greeks submissive, must time and again curry favor of their rulers and the general populace by words and gifts; whereas Diogenes cajoled no man by flattery, but told everybody the truth and, even though he possessed not a single drachma, succeeded in doing as he pleased, failed in nothing he set before himself, was the only man who lived the life he considered the best and happiest, and would not have accepted Alexander's throne or the wealth of the Medes and Persians in exchange for his own poverty.[91]

So it is clear that Diogenes appears here as the master of truth; and from this point of view, Alexander is both inferior to him and is aware of this inferiority. But although Alexander has some vices and faults of character, he is not a bad king, and he chooses to play Diogenes' parrhesiastic game:

So the king came up to Diogenes as he sat there and greeted him, whereas the other looked up at him with a terrible glare like that of a lion and ordered him to step aside a little, for Diogenes happened to be warming himself in the sun. Now Alexander was at once delighted with the man's boldness and composure in not being awestruck in his presence. For it is somehow natural for the courageous to love the courageous, while cowards eye them with misgiving and hate them as enemies, but welcome the base and like them. And so to the one class truth and frankness [*parrhesia*] are the most agreeable things in

---

91. Dio Chrysostom, "Fourth Discourse on Kingship, " Trans. J. W. Cohoon, 8–10.

the world,[92] to the other, flattery and deceit. The latter
lend a willing ear to those who in their intercourse seek to
please, the former, to those who have regard for the truth.[93]

The Cynic parrhesiastic game which begins is, in some
respects, not unlike the Socratic dialogue since there is an
exchange of questions and answers. But there are at least two
significant differences. First, in the Cynic parrhesiastic game
it is Alexander who tends to ask the questions and Diogenes,
the philosopher, who answers—which is the reverse of the
Socratic dialogue. Secondly, whereas Socrates plays with his
interlocutor's ignorance, Diogenes wants to hurt Alexander's
pride. For example, at the beginning of the exchange, Diogenes
calls Alexander a bastard [18] and tells him that someone who
claims to be a king is not so very different from a child who,
after winning a game, puts a crown on his head and declares
that he is king [47–49]. Of course, all that is not very pleasant
for Alexander to hear. But that's Diogenes' game: hitting his
interlocutor's pride, forcing him to recognize that he is not
what he claims to be—which is something quite different from
the Socratic attempt to show someone that he is ignorant of
what he claims to know. In the Socratic dialogues, you sometimes see that someone's pride has been hurt when he is compelled to recognize that he does not know what he claims to
know. For example, when Callicles is led to an awareness of his
ignorance, he renounces all discussion because his pride has
been hurt. But this is only a side effect, as it were, of the main

---

92. Diogenes Laertius notes: "Being asked what was the most beautiful
thing in the world, [Diogenes] replied 'Freedom of speech [*parrhesia*]'"
[VI, 69].
93. Dio Chrysostom, "Fourth Discourse on Kingship," 14–15.

target of Socratic irony, which is: to show someone that he is ignorant of his own ignorance. In the case of Diogenes, however, pride is the main target, and the ignorance/knowledge game is a side effect.

From these attacks on an interlocutor's pride, you see that the interlocutor is brought to the limit of the first parrhesiastic contract, viz., to agree to play the game, to choose to engage in discussion. Alexander is willing to engage Diogenes in discussion, to accept his insolence and insults, but there is a limit. And every time that Alexander feels insulted by Diogenes, he becomes angry and is close to quitting off, even to brutalizing Diogenes. So you see that the Cynic parrhesiastic game is played at the very limits of the parrhesiastic contract. It borders on transgression because the *parrhesiastes* may have made too many insulting remarks. Here is an example of this play at the limit of the parrhesiastic agreement to engage in discussion:

> …[Diogenes] went on to tell the king that he did not even possess the badge of royalty…"And what badge is that?" said Alexander. "It is the badge of the bees," he replied, "that the king wears. Have you not heard that there is a king among the bees, made so by nature, who does not hold office by virtue of what you people who trace your descent from Heracles call inheritance?" "What is this badge?" inquired Alexander. "Have you not heard farmers say," asked the other, "that this is the only bee that has no sting, since he requires no weapon against anyone? For no other bee will challenge his right to be king or fight him when he has this badge. I have an idea, however, that you not only go about fully armed but even sleep that way. Do you not know," he continued, "that it is a sign of fear

in a man for him to carry arms? And no man who is afraid would ever have a chance to become king any more than a slave would."[94]

Diogenes reasons: if you bear arms, you are afraid. No one who is afraid can be a king. So, since Alexander bears arms he cannot be a real king. And, of course, Alexander is not very pleased by this logic, and Dio continues: "At these words Alexander came near hurling his spear." That gesture, of course, would have been the rupture, the transgression, of the parrhesiastic game. When the dialogue arrives at this point, there are two possibilities available to Diogenes for bringing Alexander back into the game. One way is the following. Diogenes says, in effect, "Well, alright. I know that you are outraged and you are also free. You have both the ability and the legal sanction to kill me. But will you be courageous enough to hear the truth from me, or are you such a coward that you must kill me?" And, for example, after Diogenes insults Alexander at one point in the dialogue, he tells him:

> "...In view of what I say, rage and prance about... and think me the greatest blackguard and slander me to the world and, if it be your pleasure, run me through with your spear; for I am the only man from whom you will get the truth, and you will learn it from no one else. For all are less honest than I am and more servile." [95]

---

94. *Ibid.*, 61–64.
95. *Ibid.*, 58–59
96. *Ibid.*, 18–20.

Diogenes thus voluntarily angers Alexander, and then says, "Well, you can kill me; but if you do so, nobody else will tell you the truth." And there is an exchange, a new parrhesiastic contract is drawn up with a new limit imposed by Diogenes: either you kill me, or you'll know the truth. This kind of courageous "blackmailing" of the interlocutor in the name of truth makes a positive impression upon Alexander: "Then was Alexander amazed at the courage and fearlessness of the man" [76]. So Alexander decides to stay in the game, and a new agreement is thereby achieved.

Another means Diogenes employs for bringing Alexander back into the game is more subtle than the previous challenge: Diogenes also uses trickery. This trickery is different from Socratic irony; for, as you all know, in Socratic irony, Socrates feigns to be as ignorant as his interlocutor so that his interlocutor will not be ashamed of disclosing his own ignorance, and thus not reply to Socrates' questions. That, at least, was the principle of Socratic irony. Diogenes' trick is somewhat different; for at the moment when his interlocutor is about to terminate the exchange, Diogenes says something which his interlocutor believes is complimentary. For example, after Diogenes calls Alexander a bastard—which was not very well-received by Alexander—Diogenes tells him:

"…is it not Olympias who said that Philip is not your father, as it happens, but a dragon or Ammon or some god or other or demigod or wild animal? And yet in that case you would certainly be a bastard." Thereupon Alexander smiled and was pleased as never before, thinking that Diogenes, so far from being rude, was the most tactful of men and the only one who really knew how to pay a compliment.[96]

Whereas the Socratic dialogue traces an intricate and winding path from an ignorant understanding to an awareness of ignorance, the Cynic dialogue is much more like a fight, a battle, or a war, with peaks of great aggressivity and moments of peaceful calm—peaceful exchanges which, of course, are additional traps for the interlocutor. In the Fourth Discourse Dio Chrysostom explains the rationale behind this strategy of mixing aggressivity and sweetness; Diogenes asks Alexander:

"Have you not heard the Libyan myth?"[97] And the king replied that he had not. Then Diogenes told it to him with zest and charm, because he wanted to put him in a good humor, just as nurses, after giving the children a whipping, tell them a story to comfort and please them.[98]

And a bit further on, Dio adds:

When Diogenes perceived that [Alexander] was greatly excited and quite keyed up in mind with expectancy, he toyed with him and pulled him about in the hope that somehow he might be moved from his pride and thirst for glory and be able to sober up a little. For he noticed that at one moment he was delighted, and at another grieved, at the same thing, and that his soul was as unsettled as the weather at the solstices when both rain and sunshine come from the very same cloud.[99]

Diogenes' charm, however, is only a means of advancing

---

97. Cf. Dio Chrysostom, "The Fifth Discourse: A Libyan Myth."
98. Dio Chrysostom, "The Fourth Discourse on Kingship," 73–74.
99. *Ibid.*, 77–78.

the game and of preparing the way for additional aggressive exchanges. Thus, after Diogenes pleases Alexander with his remarks about his "bastard" genealogy, and considers the possibility that Alexander might be the son of Zeus, he goes even further: he tells Alexander that when Zeus has a son, he gives his son marks of his divine birth. Of course, Alexander thinks that he has such marks. Alexander then asks Diogenes how one can be a good king. And Diogenes' reply is a purely moral portrayal of kingship:

> "No one can be a bad king any more than he can be a bad good man; for the king is the best one among men, since he is most brave and righteous and humane, and cannot be overcome by any toil or by any appetite. Or do you think a man is a charioteer if he cannot drive, or that one is a pilot if he is ignorant of steering, or is a physician if he knows not how to cure? It is impossible, nay, though all the Greeks and barbarians acclaim him as such and load him with diadems and sceptres and tiaras like so many necklaces that are put on castaway children lest they fail of recognition. Therefore, just as one cannot pilot except after the manner of pilots, so no one can be king except in a kingly way."[100]

We see here the analogy of statesmanship with navigation and medicine that we have already noted. As the "son of Zeus," Alexander thinks that he has marks or signs to show that he is a king with a divine birth. But Diogenes shows Alexander that the truly royal character is not linked to special

---

100. *Ibid.,* 24–25.

status, birth, power, and so on. Rather, the only way of being a true king is to behave like one. And when Alexander asks how he might learn this art of kingship, Diogenes tells him that it cannot be learned, for one is noble by nature [26–31].

Here the game reaches a point where Alexander does not become conscious of his lack of knowledge, as in a Socratic dialogue. He discovers, instead, that he is not in any way what he thought he was—viz., a king by royal birth, with marks of his divine status, or king because of his superior power, and so on. He is brought to a point where Diogenes tells him that the only way to be a real king is to adopt the same type of *ethos* as the Cynic philosopher. And at this point in the exchange there is nothing more for Alexander to say.

In the case of Socratic dialogue, it also sometimes happens that when the person Socrates has been questioning no longer knows what to say, Socrates resumes the discourse by presenting a positive thesis, and then the dialogue ends. In this text by Dio Chrysostom, Diogenes begins a continuous discourse; however, his discussion does not present the truth of a positive thesis, but is content to give a precise description of three faulty modes of life linked to the royal character. The first one is devoted to wealth, the second to physical pleasure, and the third to glory and political power. And these three life-styles are personified by three *daimones* or spirits.

The concept of the *daimon* was popular in Greek culture, and also became a philosophical concept—in Plutarch, for example. The fight against evil *daimones* in Christian asceticism has precursors in the Cynic tradition. Incidentally, the concept of the *démon* has been elaborated in an excellent article in the *Dictionnaire de Spiritualité*.[101]

---

101. Cf. Francois Vandenbroucke, "Démon," *Dictionnaire de Spiritualité*.

Diogenes gives an indication of the three *daimones* which Alexander must fight throughout his life, and which constitute the target of a permanent "spiritual struggle"—*"combat spirituel."* Of course, this phrase does not occur in Dio's text; for here it is not so much a content which is specific and important, but the idea of a parrhesiastic practice which enables someone to fight a spiritual war within himself.

And I think we can also see in the aggressive encounter between Alexander and Diogenes a struggle occurring between two kinds of power: political power and the power of truth. In this struggle, the *parrhesiastes* accepts and confronts a permanent danger: Diogenes exposes himself to Alexander's power from the beginning to the end of the Discourse. And the main effect of this parrhesiastic struggle with power is not to bring the interlocutor to a new truth, or to a new level of self-awareness; it is to lead the interlocutor to *internalize* this parrhesiastic struggle—to fight within himself against his own faults, and to be with himself in the same way that Diogenes was with him.

Personal relationships [102]

I would now like to analyze the parrhesiastic game in the framework of personal relationships, selecting some examples from Plutarch and Galen which I think illustrate some of the technical problems which can arise.

In Plutarch there is a text which is explicitly devoted to the problem of *parrhesia.* Addressing certain aspects of the parrhesiastic problem, Plutarch tries to answer the question: How is it possible to recognize a true *parrhesiastes* or truth-teller? And similarly: How is it possible to distinguish a *parrhesiastes*

---

102. Sixth and Final Lecture: 30 November 1983.

from a flatterer? The title of this text, which cames from Plutarch's *Moralia*, is "How to Tell a Flatterer from a Friend."[103]

I think we need to underline several points from this essay. First, why do we need, in our personal lives, to have some friend who plays the role of a *parrhesiastes*, of a truth-teller? The reason Plutarch gives is found in the predominant kind of relationship we often have to ourselves, viz., a relation of *philautia* [φιλαυτία] or "self-love." This relation of self-love is, for us, the ground of a persistent illusion about what we really are:

> It is because of this self-love that everybody is himself his own foremost and greatest flatterer, and hence finds no difficulty in admitting the outsider to witness with him and to confirm his own conceits and desires. For the man who is spoken of with opprobrium as a lover of flatterers is in high degree a lover of self, and, because of his kindly feeling towards himself, he desires and conceives himself to be endowed with all manner of good qualities; but although the desire for these is not unnatural, yet the conceit that one possesses them is dangerous and must be carefully avoided. Now if Truth is a thing divine, and, as Plato puts it, the origin "of all good for gods and all good for men" [*Laws*, 730c], then the flatterer is in all likelihood an enemy to the gods and particularly to the Pythian god. For the flatterer always takes a position over against the maxim "Know Thyself," by creating in every man deception towards himself and ignorance both of

103. Plutarch, "How to Tell a Flatterer from a Friend," Trans. F. C. Babbitt. *Moralia*, Vol. 1, 261–395.

himself and of the good and evil that concerns himself; the good he renders defective and incomplete, and the evil wholly impossible to amend.[104]

We are our own flatterers, and it is in order to disconnect this spontaneous relation we have to ourselves, to rid ourselves of our *philautia,* that we need a *parrhesiastes.*

But it is difficult to *recognize* and to *accept* a *parrhesiastes.* For not only is it difficult to distinguish a true *parrhesiastes* from a flatterer; because of our *philautia* we are also not *interested* in recognizing a *parrhesiastes.* So at stake in this text is the problem of determining the indubitable criteria which enable us to distinguish the genuine *parrhesiastes* we need so badly to rid ourselves of our own *philautia* from the flatterer who "plays the part of friend with the gravity of a tragedian" [50e].[105] And this implies that we are in posession of a kind of "semi-

---

104. *Ibid.,* 49a–b.
105. Regarding the strategies the flatterer employs to camouflage his true nature, Plutarch writes: "The most unprincipled trick of all that he has is this: perceiving that frankness of speech [*parrhesia*], by common report and belief, is the language of friendship especially (as an animal has its peculiar cry), and, on the other hand, that lack of frankness is unfriendly and ignoble, he does not allow even this to escape imitation, but, just as clever cooks employ bitter extracts and astringent flavorings to remove the cloying effect of sweet things, so flatterers apply a frankness which is not genuine or beneficial, but which, as it were, winks while it frowns, and does nothing but tickle. For these reasons, then, the man is hard to detect, as in the case with some animals to which Nature has given the faculty of changing their hue, so that they exactly conform to the colors and objects beneath them. And since the flatterer uses resemblances to deceive and to wrap about him, it is our task to use the differences in order to unwrap him and lay him bare, in the act, as Plato puts it, of 'adorning himself with alien colors and forms for want of any of his own' [*Phaedrus*, 239d]" (51c–d).

ology" of the real *parrhesiastes*.

Plutarch proposes two major criteria to answer the question, How can we recognize a true *parrhesiastes?* First, there is a conformity between what the real truth-teller says with how he behaves—and here you recognize the Socratic harmony of the *Laches*, where Laches explains that he could trust Socrates as a truth-teller about courage since he saw that Socrates really *was* courageous at Delium, and thus, that he exhibited a harmonious accord between what he said and what he did.

There is also a second criterion, which is: the permanence, the continuity, the stability and steadiness of the true *parrhesiastes*, the true friend, regarding his choices, his opinions, and his thoughts:

> ...it is necessary to observe the uniformity and permanence of his tastes, whether he always takes delight in the same things, and commends always the same things, and whether he directs and ordains his own life according to one pattern, as becomes a freeborn man and a lover of congenial friendship and intimacy; for such is the conduct of a friend. But the flatterer, since he has no abiding place of character to dwell in, and since he leads a life not of his own choosing but another's, molding and adapting himself to suit another, is not simple, not one, but variable and many in one, and, like water that is poured into one receptacle after another, he is constantly on the move from place to place, and changes his shape to fit his receiver.[106]

---

106. Plutarch, "How to Tell a Flatterer from a Friend," 52a–b.

Of course there are a lot of other very interesting things about this essay. But I would like to underscore two major themes. First, the theme of *self-delusion*, and its link with *philautia*—which is not something completely new. But in Plutarch's text you can see that his notion of self-delusion as a consequence of self-love is clearly different from being in a state of ignorance about one's own lack of self-knowledge—a state which Socrates attempted to overcome. Plutarch's conception emphasizes the fact that not only are we unable to know that we know nothing, but we are also unable to know exactly what we are. And I think that this theme of self-delusion becomes increasingly important in Hellenistic culture. In Plutarch's period it is something really significant.

A second theme which I would like to stress is steadiness of mind. This is also not something new, but for late Stoicism the notion of steadiness takes on great importance. And there is an obvious relation between these two themes—the theme of self-delusion and the theme of constancy or persistency [ἐνδελέχεια] of mind. For destroying self-delusion and acquiring and maintaining continuity of mind are two ethico-moral activities which are linked to one another. The self-delusion which prevents you from knowing who or what you are, and all the shifts in your thoughts, feelings, and opinions which force you to move from one thought to another, one feeling to another, or one opinion to another, demonstrate this linkage. For if you are able to discern exactly what you are, then you will stick to the same point, and you will not be moved by anything. If you are moved by any sort of stimulation, feeling, passion, etc., then you are not able to stay close to yourself, you are dependent upon something else, you are driven to different concerns, and consequently you are not able to maintain complete self-possession.

These two elements—being deluded about yourself and being moved by changes in the world and in your thoughts—both developed and gained significance in the Christian tradition. In early Christian spirituality, Satan is often represented as the agent both of self-delusion (as opposed to the renunciation of self) and of the mobility of mind—the instability or unsteadiness of the soul as opposed to *firmitas* in the contemplation of God. Fastening one's mind to God was a way, first, of renouncing one's self so as to eliminate any kind of self-delusion.[107] And it was also a way to acquire an ethical and an ontological steadiness. So I think that we can see in Plutarch's text—in the analysis of the relation between *parrhesia* and flattery—some elements which also became significant for the Christian tradition.

I would like to refer now, very briefly, to a text by Galen [A.D. 130–200]—the famous physician at the end of the Second Century—where you can see the same problem: How is it possible to recognize a real *parrhesiastes?* Galen raises this question in his essay "The Diagnosis and Cure of the Soul's Passions," where he explains that in order for a man to free himself from his passions, he needs a *parrhesiastes;* for just as in Plutarch a century previously, *philautia,* self-love, is the root of self-delusion:

> ...we see the faults of others but remain blind to those which concern ourselves. All men admit the truth of this and, furthermore, Plato gives the reason for it [*Laws,* 731e]. He says that the lover is blind in the case of the object of his love. If, therefore, each of us loves himself most of all, he must be blind in his own case...
>
> There are passions of the soul which everybody knows: anger, wrath, fear, grief, envy, and violent lust. In

my opinion, excessive vehemence in loving or hating anything is also a passion; I think the saying "moderation is
best" is correct, since no immoderate action is good. How,
then, could a man cut out these passions if he did not first
know that he had them? But as we said, it is impossible to

---

107. Foucault discusses the Christian "renunciation of self" in the context
of Christian truth obligations in the following: "What about truth as
a duty in our Christian societies? As everybody knows, Christianity is
a confession. This means that Christianity belongs to a very special type
of religion–those which impose obligations of truth on those who practice
them. Such obligations in Christianity are numerous. For instance, there
is the obligation to hold as truth a set of propositions which constitute
dogma, the obligation to hold certain books as a permanent source of
truth, and obligations to accept the decisions of certain authorities in matters of truth. But Christianity requires another form of truth obligation.
Everyone in Christianity has the duty to explore who he is, what is hap-
pening within himself, the faults he may have committed, the temptations
to which he is exposed. Moreover everyone is obliged to tell these things
to other people, and hence to bear witness against himself.

"These two ensembles of obligation—those regarding the faith, the
book, the dogma, and those regarding the self, the soul, and the heart—
are linked together. A Christian needs the light of faith when he wants to
explore himself. Conversely, his access to the truth can't be conceived of
without the purification of the soul... I would like to underline that the
Christian discovery of the self does not reveal the self as an illusion.
It gives place to a task which can't be anything else but undefined. This
task has two objectives. First, there is the task of clearing up all the illusions, temptations, and seductions which can occur in the mind, and discovering the reality of what is going on within ourselves. Secondly, one
has to get free from any attachment to this self, not because the self is an
illusion, but because the self is much too real. The more we discover the
truth about ourselves, the more we have to renounce ourselves; and the
more we want to renounce ourselves, the more we need to bring to light
the reality of ourselves. That is what we could call the spiral of truth formulation and reality renouncement which is at the heart of Christian
techniques of the self" ["Sexuality and Solitude," *London Review of Books*,
21 May–3 June 1981, 5].

know them, since we love ourselves to excess. Even if this saying will not permit you to judge yourself, it does allow that you can judge others whom you neither love nor hate. Whenever you hear anyone in town being praised because he flatters no man, associate with that man and judge from your own experience whether he is the sort of man they say he is...

When a man does not greet the powerful and wealthy by name, when he does not visit them, when he does not dine with them, when he lives a disciplined life, expect that man to speak the truth; try, too, to come to a deeper knowledge of what kind of man he is (and this comes about through long association). If you find such a man, summon him and talk with him one day in private; ask him to reveal straightaway whatever of the abovementioned passions he may see in you. Tell him you will be most grateful for this service and that you will look on him as your deliverer more than if he had saved you from an illness of the body. Have him promise to reveal it whenever he sees you affected by any of the passions I have mentioned.[108]

It is interesting to note that in this text, the *parrhesiastes*—which everyone needs in order to get rid of his own self-delusion—does not need to be a friend, someone you know, someone with whom you are acquainted. And this, I think, constitutes a very important difference between Galen and Plutarch. In Plutarch, Seneca, and the tradition which derives from

---

108. Galen, "The Diagnosis and Cure of the Soul's Passions," Trans. Paul W. Harkins; 31–33.

Socrates, the *parrhesiastes* always needs to be a friend. And this friendship relation was always at the root of the parrhesiastic game. As far as I know, for the first time with Galen, the *parrhesiastes* no longer needs to be a friend. Indeed, it is much better, Galen tells us, that the *parrhesiastes* be someone whom you do not know in order for him to be completely *neutral*. A good truth-teller who gives you honest counsel about yourself does not hate you, but he does not love you either. A good *parrhesiastes* is someone with whom you have previously had no particular relationship.

But of course you cannot choose him at random. You must check some criteria in order to know whether he really is capable of revealing your faults. And for this you must have heard of him. Does he have a good reputation? Is he old enough? Is he rich enough? It is very important that the one who plays the role of the *parrhesiastes* be at least as rich as, or richer than, you are. For if he is poor and you are rich, then the chances will be greater that he will be a flatterer, since it is now in his interest to do so.[109]

The Cynics, of course, would have said that someone who is rich, who has a positive relation to wealth, cannot really be wise; so it is not worthwhile selecting him as a *parrhesiastes*. Galen's idea of selecting someone who is richer than you to act as your truth-teller would seem ridiculous to a Cynic.

But it is also interesting to note that in this essay, the truth-teller does not need to be a physician or doctor. For in spite of the fact that Galen himself was a physician, was often obliged to "cure" the excessive passions of others, and often succeeded

---

109. *Ibid.*, 32–36; cf. Michel Foucault, *Le Souci de soi*, 65–69, 72.

in doing so, he does not require of a *parrhesiastes* that he be a doctor, or that he possess the ability to cure you of your passions. All that is required is that he be able to tell you the truth about yourself.

But it is still not enough to know that the truth-teller is old enough, rich enough, and has a good reputation. He must also be *tested.* And Galen gives a program for testing the potential *parrhesiastes.* For example, you must ask him questions about himself and see how he responds to determine whether he will be severe enough for the role. You have to be suspicious when the would-be *parrhesiastes* congratulates you, when he is *not* severe enough, and so on.

Galen does not elaborate upon the precise role of the *parrhesiastes* in " The Diagnosis and Cure of the Soul's Passions"; he only gives a few examples of the sort of advice he himself gave while assuming this role for others. But, to summarize the foregoing, in this text the relationship between *parrhesia* and friendship no longer seems to obtain, and there is a kind of trial or examination required of the potential *parrhesiastes* by his "patron" or "client."

I apologize for being so brief about these texts from Plutarch and Galen; but they are not very difficult to read, only difficult to find.

In Techniques of Examination
Preliminary remarks

I would now like to turn to the various techniques of the parrhesiastic games which can be found in the philosophical and moral literature of the first two centuries of our era. Of course, I do not plan to enumerate or discuss all of the important practices that can be found in the writings of this period. To begin with, I would like to make three preliminary remarks.

First, I think that these techniques manifest a very interesting and important shift from that truth game which—in the
classical Greek conception of *parrhesia*—was constituted by
the fact that someone was courageous enough to tell the truth
to *other people*. For there is a shift from *that* kind of parrhesiastic game to another truth game which now consists in being
courageous enough to disclose the truth about *oneself*.

Secondly, this new kind of parrhesiastic game—where
the problem is to confront the truth about yourself—requires
what the Greeks called *askesis* [ἄσκεσις]. Although our word
asceticism derives from the Greek word *askesis* (since the meaning of the word changes as it becomes associated with various
Christian practices), for the Greeks the word does not mean
"ascetic," but has a very broad sense denoting *any* kind of
practical training or exercise. For example, it was a commonplace to say that any kind of art or technique had to be learned
by *mathesis* and *askesis*—by theoretical knowledge and practical training. And, for instance, when Musonius Rufus says
that the art of living, *techne tou biou,* is like the other arts, i.e.,
an art which one could not learn only through theoretical
teachings, he is repeating a traditional doctrine. This *techne tou
biou,* this art of living, demands practice and training: *askesis.*[110] But the Greek conception of *askesis* differs from
Christian ascetic practices in at least two ways: (1) Christian
asceticism has as its ultimate aim or target the renunciation of
the self, whereas the moral *askesis* of the Greco-Roman

---

110. Cf. Musonius Rufus, "On Training" [Περὶ ἀσηησεως], 53–57;
Epictetus, "On Training," in *The Discourses as Reported by Arrian* (III, 12);
Michel Foucault, *The Care of the Self* (Chapter II: The Culture of the Self);
Foucault interview, "On the Genealogy of Ethics," *passim;* P. Hadot,
Exercises spirituels et philosophie antique.

philosophies has as its goal the establishment of a specific relationship to oneself—a relationship of self-possession and self-sovereignty; (2) Christian asceticism takes as its principal theme detachment from the world, whereas the ascetic practices of the Greco-Roman philosophies are generally concerned with endowing the individual with the preparation and the moral equipment that will permit him to fully confront the world in an ethical and rational manner.

Thirdly, these ascetic practices implied numerous different kinds of specific exercises; but they were never specifically catalogued, analyzed, or described. Some of them were discussed and criticized, but most of them were well-known. Since most people recognized them, they were usually used without any precise theory about the exercise. And indeed, when one now reads these Greek and Latin authors as they discuss such exercises in the context of specific theoretical topics (such as time, death, the world, life, necessity, etc.), one often gets a mistaken conception about them. For these topics usually function only as a schema or matrix for the spiritual exercise. In fact, most of these texts written in late antiquity about ethics are not at all concerned with advancing a theory about the foundations of ethics, but are practical books containing specific recipes and exercises one had to read, to reread, to meditate upon, to learn, in order to construct a lasting matrix for one's own behavior.

I now turn to the kinds of exercises where someone had to examine the truth about himself, and tell this truth to someone else.

Most of the time when we refer to such exercises, we speak of practices involving the "examination of conscience." But I think that the expression "examination of conscience" as a blanket term meant to characterize all these different exercises misleads and oversimplifies. For we have to define very precisely the different truth games which have been put into work and applied in these practices of the Greco-Roman tradition. I would like to analyze five of these truth games commonly described as "examinations of conscience" in order to show you (1) how some of the exercises differ from one another; (2) what aspects of the mind, feelings, behavior, etc., were considered in these different exercises; and (3) that these exercises, despite their differences, implied a relation between truth and the self which is very different from what we find in the Christian tradition.

Solitary self-examination

The first text I would like to analyze comes from Seneca's *De ira* ["On Anger"]:

> All our senses ought to be trained to endurance. They are naturally long-suffering, if only the mind desists from weakening them. This should be summoned to give an account of itself every day. Sextius had this habit, and when the day was over and he had retired to his nightly rest, he would put these questions to his soul: "What bad habit have you cured today? What fault have you resisted? In what respects are you better?" Anger will cease and become controllable if it finds that it must appear before a judge every day. Can anything be more excellent that this practice of thoroughly sifting the whole day? And how delightful the sleep that follows this self-examination—how tranquil it is, how deep and untroubled, when the soul has either praised or admonished itself, and when this secret examiner and critic of self has given report of its own character! I avail myself of this privilege,

and every day I plead my cause before the bar of self. When the light has been removed from sight, and my wife, long aware of my habit, has become silent, I scan the whole of my day and retrace all my deeds and words.

I conceal nothing from myself, I omit nothing. For why should I shrink from any of my mistakes, when I may commune thus with my self? "See that you never do that again; I will pardon you this time. In that dispute you spoke too offensively; after this don't have encounters with ignorant people; those who have never learned do not want to learn. You reproved that man more frankly than you ought, and consequently you have not so much mended him as offended him. In the future, consider not only the truth of what you say, but also whether the man to whom you are speaking can endure the truth. A good man accepts reproof gladly; the worse a man is the more bitterly he resents it."[111]

We know from several sources that this kind of exercise was a daily requirement, or at least a habit, in the Pythagorean tradition.[112] Before they went to sleep, the Pythagoreans had to perform this kind of examination, recollecting the faults they had committed during the day. Such faults consisted in those sorts of behavior which transgressed the very strict rules of the Pythagorean Schools. And the purpose of this examination, at least in the Pythagorean tradition, was to purify the soul. Such purification was believed necessary since the Pythagoreans considered sleep to be a state of being whereby the soul could

---

111. Seneca, "On Anger," Trans. John W. Basore; 338–341.
112. Cf. Michel Foucault, *Le Souci de soi*, 77.

get in contact with the divinity through dreams. And, of course, one had to keep one's soul as pure as possible both to have beautiful dreams, and also to come into contact with benevolent deities. In this text of Seneca's we can clearly see that this Pythagorean tradition survives in the exercise he describes (as it also does later on in similar practices utilized by the Christians). The idea of employing sleep and dreams as a possible means of apprehending the divine can also be found in Plato's *Republic* [Book IX, 571e–572b]. Seneca tells us that by means of this exercise we are able to procure good and delightful sleep: "How delightful the sleep that follows this examination—how tranquil it is, how deep and untroubled." And we know from Seneca himself that under his teacher, Sotio, his first training was partly Pythagorean. Seneca relates this practice, however, not to Pythagorean custom, but to Quintus Sextius, who was one of the advocates of Stoicism in Rome at the end of the First Century B.C. And it seems that this exercise, despite its purely Pythagorean origin, was utilized and praised by several philosophical sects and schools: the Epicureans, Stoics, Cynics, and others. There are references in Epictetus, for example, to this kind of exercise. And it would be useless to deny that Seneca's self-examination is similar to the kinds of ascetic practices used for centuries in the Christian tradition. But if we look at the text more closely, I think we can see some interesting differences.[113]

First, there is the question of Seneca's attitude towards himself. What kind of operation is Seneca actually performing in this exercise? What is the practical matrix he uses and applies in relation to himself? At first glance, it seems to be

---

113. *Ibid.*, 77ff.

a judiciary practice which is close to the Christian confessional: there are thoughts, these thoughts are confessed, there is an accused (namely, Seneca), there is an accuser or prosecutor (who is also Seneca), there is a judge (also Seneca), and it seems that there is a verdict. The entire scene seems to be judiciary; and Seneca employs typical judiciary expressions ("appear before a judge," "plead my cause before the bar of self," etc.). Closer scrutiny shows, however, that it is a question of something different from the court, or from judicial procedure. For instance, Seneca says that he is an "examiner" of himself [*speculator sui*]. The word *speculator* means an "examiner" or "inspector"—typically someone who inspects the freight on a ship, or the work being done by builders constructing a house, etc. Seneca also says *"totum diem meum scrutor"*—"I examine, inspect, the whole of my day." Here the verb *scrutor* belongs, not to judicial vocabulary, but to the vocabulary of administration. Seneca states further on: *"factaque ac dicta mea remetior"*—"and I retrace, recount, all my deeds and words." The verb *remetiri* is a technical term used in bookkeeping and has the sense of checking whether there is any kind of miscalculation or error in the accounts. So Seneca is not exactly a judge passing sentence upon himself. He is much more of an *administrator* who, once the work is finished, or when the year's business is completed, draws up the accounts, takes stock of things, and sees whether everything has been done correctly. It is more of an administrative scene than a judiciary one.

And if we turn to the faults that Seneca retraces, and which he gives as examples in this examination, we can see that they are not the sort of faults we would call "sins." He does not confess, for example, that he drinks too much, or has committed financial fraud, or has bad feelings for someone else—faults Seneca was very familiar with as one of Nero's ring. He reproaches himself for very different things. He has criticized someone, but instead of his criticism helping the man, it has hurt him. Or he criticizes himself for being disgusted by people who were, in any case, incapable of understanding him. Behaving in such fashion, he commits "mistakes" [*errores*]; but these mistakes are only inefficient actions requiring adjustments between ends and means. He criticizes himself for not keeping the aim of his actions in mind, for not seeing that it is useless to blame someone if the criticism given will not improve things, and so on. The point of the fault concerns a *practical* error in his behavior since he was unable to establish an effective rational relation between the principles of conduct he knows and the behavior he actually engaged in. Seneca's faults are not transgressions of a code or law. They express, rather, occasions when his attempt to coordinate rules of behavior (rules he already accepts, recognizes, and knows) with his own actual behavior in a specific situation has proven to be unsuccessful or inefficient.

Seneca also does not *react* to his own errors as if they were sins. He does not punish himself; there is nothing like penance. The retracing of his mistakes has as its object the reactivation of practical rules of behavior which, now reinforced, may be useful for future occasions. He thus tells himself: "See that you never do that again," "Don't have encounters with ignorant people," "In the future, consider not only the truth of what you say, but also whether the man to whom you are speaking can endure the truth," and so on. Seneca does not analyze his responsibility or feelings of guilt; it is not, for him, a question of purifying himself of these faults. Rather, he engages in a kind of administrative scrutiny which enables him to reactivate various rules and maxims in order to make them more vivid, permanent, and effective for future behavior.

Self-diagnosis

The second text I would like to discuss comes from Seneca's *De tranquillitate animi* ["On the Tranquillity of Mind"]. The *De tranquillitate animi* is one of a number of texts written about a theme we have already encountered, viz., constancy or steadiness of mind. To put it very briefly, the Latin word *tranquillitas,* which is supposed to translate the Greek word εὐθυμία, denotes stability of soul or mind. It is a state where the mind is independent of any kind of external event, and is free as well from any internal excitation or agitation that could induce an involuntary movement of mind. Thus it denotes stability, self-sovereignty, and independence. But *tranquillitas* also refers to a certain feeling of pleasurable calm which has its source, its principle, in this self-sovereignty or self-possession of the self.

At the beginning of the *De tranquillitate animi,* Annaeus Serenus asks Seneca for a consultation. Serenus is a young friend of Seneca's who belonged to the same family, and who started his political career under Nero as Nero's nightwatchman. For both Seneca and Serenus there is no incompatibility between philosophy and a political career since a philosophical life is not merely an alternative to a political life. Rather, philosophy must accompany a political life in order to provide a moral framework for public activity. Serenus, who was initially an Epicurean, later turned towards Stoicism. But even after he became a Stoic, he felt uncomfortable; for he had the impression that he was not able to improve himself, that he had reached a dead end, and was unable to make any progress.

I should note that for the Old Stoa—for Zeno of Citium, for example—when a person knew the doctrines of the Stoic philosophy he did not really need to progress anymore, for he has thereby succeeded in becoming a Stoic. What is interesting here is the idea of progress occurring as a new development in the evolution of Stoicism. Serenus knows the Stoic doctrine and its practical rules, but still lacks *tranquillitas*. And it is in this state of unrest that he turns to Seneca and asks him for help. Of course, we cannot be sure that this depiction of Serenus' state reflects his real historical situation; we can only be reasonably sure that Seneca wrote this text. But the text is supposed to be a letter written to Serenus incorporating the latter's request for moral advice. And it exhibits a model or pattern for a type of self-examination.

Serenus examines what he is or what he has accomplished at the moment when he requests this consultation:

SERENUS: When I made examination of myself, it became evident, Seneca, that some of my vices are uncovered and displayed so openly that I can put my hand upon them, some are more hidden and lurk in a corner, some are not always present but recur at intervals; and I should say that the last are by far the most troublesome, being like roving enemies that spring upon one when the opportunity offers, and allow one neither to be ready as in war, nor to be off guard as in peace.

Nevertheless the state in which I find myself most of all—for why should I not admit the truth to you as to a physician?—is that I have neither been honestly set free from the things I hated and feared, nor, on the other hand, am I in bondage to them; while the condition in which I am placed is not the worst, yet I am complaining and fretful—I am neither sick nor well.[114]

As you can see, Serenus' request takes the form of a "medical" consultation of his own spiritual state. For he says, "why should I not admit the truth to you as to a physician?"; "I am neither sick nor well"; and so on. These expressions are clearly related to the well-known metaphorical identification of moral discomfort with physical illness. And what is also important to underline here is that in order for Serenus to be cured of his illness, he first needs to "admit the truth" [verum fatear] to Seneca. But what are the truths that Serenus must "confess"?

We shall see that he discloses no secret faults, no shameful desires, nothing like that. It is something entirely different from a Christian confession. And this "confession" can be divided into two parts. First, there is Serenus' very general exposé about himself; and secondly, there is an exposé of his attitude in different fields of activity in his life.

The general exposé about his condition is the following:

There is no need for you to say that all the virtues are weakly at the beginning, that firmness and strength are added by time. I am well aware also that the virtues that struggle for outward show, I mean for position and the fame of eloquence and all that comes under the verdict of others, do grow stronger as time passes—both those that provide real strength and those that trick us out with a sort of dye with a view to pleasing, must wait long years until gradually length of time develops color—but I greatly fear that

---

114. Seneca, "On Tranquillity of Mind," Trans. John W. Basore, I. 1–3.

habit, which brings stability to most things, may cause this fault of mine to become more deeply implanted. Of things evil as well as good long intercourse induces love.

The nature of this weakness of mind that halts between two things and inclines strongly neither to the right nor to the wrong, I cannot show you so well all at once as a part at a time; I shall tell you what befalls me— you will find a name for my malady.[115]

Serenus tells us that the truth about himself that he will now expose is descriptive of the malady he suffers from. And from these general remarks and other indications he gives later on, we can see that this malady is compared throughout to the seasickness caused by being aboard a boat which no longer advances, but rolls and pitches at sea. Serenus is afraid of remaining at sea in this condition, in full view of the dry land which remains inaccessible to him. The organization of the themes Serenus describes, with its implicit and, as we shall see, its explicit metaphorical reference to being at sea, involves the traditional association in moral-political philosophy of medicine and piloting a boat or navigation—which we have already seen. Here we also have the same three elements: a moral-philosophical problem, reference to medicine, and reference to piloting. Serenus is on the way towards acquiring the truth like a ship at sea in sight of dry land. But because he lacks complete self-possession or self-mastery, he has the feeling that he cannot advance. Perhaps because he is too weak, perhaps his course is not a good one. He does not know exactly what is the reason for his waverings, but he characterizes his *malaise* as a kind of perpetual vacillating motion which has no

---

115. Seneca, "On the Tranquillity of Mind," I. 3–4.

other movement than "rocking." The boat cannot advance
because it is rocking. So Serenus' problem is: how can he
replace this wavering motion of rocking—which is due to the
instability, the unsteadiness of his mind—with a steady linear
movement that will take him to the coast and to the firm
earth? It is a problem of dynamics, but very different from the
Freudian dynamics of an unconscious conflict between two
psychic forces. Here we have an oscillating motion of rocking
which prevents the movement of the mind from advancing
towards the truth, towards steadiness, towards the ground.
And now we have to see how this metaphorical dynamic grid
organizes Serenus' description of himself in the following long
quotation:

> (l) I am possessed by the very greatest love of frugality,
> I must confess; I do not like a couch made up for display,
> nor clothing brought forth from a chest or pressed by
> weights and a thousand mangles to make it glossy, but
> homely and cheap, that is neither preserved nor to be put
> on with anxious care; the food that I like is neither pre-
> pared nor watched by a household of slaves, it does not
> need to be ordered many days before nor to be served by
> many hands, but is easy to get and abundant; there is
> nothing far-fetched or costly about it, nowhere will there
> be any lack of it, it is burdensome neither to the purse nor
> to the body, nor will it return by the way it entered; the
> servant that I like is a young home-born slave without
> training or skill; the silver is my country-bred father's
> heavy plate bearing no stamp of the maker's name, and
> the table is not notable for the variety of its markings or
> known to the town from the many fashionable owners
> through whose hands it has passed, but one that stands

for use, and will neither cause the eyes of any guest to linger upon it with pleasure nor fire them with envy. Then, after all these things have had my full approval, my mind [*animus*] is dazzled by the magnificence of some training schools for pages, by the sight of slaves bedecked with gold and more carefully arrayed than the leaders of a public procession, and a whole regiment of glittering attendants; by the sight of a house where one even treads on precious stones and riches are scattered about in every corner, where the very roofs glitter, and the whole town pays court and escorts an inheritance on the road to ruin. And what shall I say of the waters, transparent to the bottom, that flow around the guests even as they banquet, what of the feasts that are worthy of their setting? Coming from a long abandonment to thrift, luxury has poured around me the wealth of its splendor, and echoed around me on every side. My sight falters a little, for I can lift up my heart towards it more easily than my eyes. And so I come back, not worse, but sadder, and I do not walk among my paltry possessions with head erect as before, and there enters a secret sting and the doubt whether the other life is not better. None of these things changes me, yet none of them fails to disturb me.

(2) I resolve to obey the commands of my teachers and plunge into the midst of public life; I resolve to try to gain office and the consulship, attracted of course, not by the purple or by the lictor's rods, but by the desire to be more serviceable and useful to my friends and relatives and all my countrymen and then to all mankind. Ready and determined, I follow Zeno, Cleanthes, and Chrysippus, of whom none the less not one failed to urge others to do so.

And then, whenever something upsets my mind, which is unused to meeting shocks, whenever something happens that is either unworthy of me, and many such occur in the lives of all human beings, or that does not proceed very easily, or when things that are not to be accounted of great value demand much of my time, I turn back to my leisure, and just as wearied flocks too do, I quicken my pace towards home. I resolve to confine my life within its own walls: "Let no one," I say, "who will make me no worthy return for such a loss rob me of a single day; let my mind be fixed upon itself, let it cultivate itself, let it busy itself with nothing outside, nothing that looks towards an umpire; let it love the tranquillity that is remote from public and private concern." But when my mind [*animus*] has been aroused by reading of great bravery, and noble examples have applied the spur, I want to rush into the forum, to lend my voice to one man; to offer such assistance to another as, even if it will not help, will be an effort to help; or to check the pride of someone in the forum who has been unfortunately puffed up by his successes.

(3) And in my literary studies I think that it is surely better to fix my eyes on the theme itself, and, keeping this uppermost when I speak, to trust meanwhile to the theme to supply the words so that unstudied language may follow it wherever it leads. I say: "What need is there to compose something that will last for centuries? Will you not give up striving to keep posterity silent about you? You were born for death; a silent funeral is less troublesome! And so to pass the time, write something in simple style, for your own use, not for publication; they that study for

the day have less need to labor." Then again, when my
mind [*animus*] has been uplifted by the greatness of its
thoughts, it becomes ambitious of words, and with higher aspirations it desires higher expression, and language
issues forth to match the dignity of the theme; forgetful
then of my rule and of my more restrained judgment,
I am swept to loftier heights by an utterance that is no
longer my own.

Not to indulge longer in details, I am all things attended
by this weakness of good intention. In fact I fear that I am
gradually losing ground, or, what causes me even more
worry, that I am hanging like one who is always on the
verge of falling, and that perhaps I am in a more serious
condition than I myself perceive; for we take a favorable
view of our private matters, and partiality always ham-
pers our judgment. I fancy that many men would have
arrived at wisdom if they had not fancied that they had
already arrived, if they had not dissembled about certain
traits in their character and passed by others with their
eyes shut. For there is no reason for you to suppose that
the adulation of other people is more ruinous to us than
our own. Who dares to tell himself the truth? Who,
though he is surrounded by a horde of applauding syco-
phants, is not for all that his own greatest flatterer? I beg
you, therefore, if you have any remedy by which you
could stop this fluctuation of mine, to deem me worthy of
being indebted to you for tranquillity. I know that these
mental disturbances of mine are not dangerous and give
no promise of a storm; to express what I complain of in
apt metaphor, I am distressed, not by a tempest, but by
sea-sickness. Do you, then, take from me this trouble,

whatever it be, and rush to the rescue of one who is strug-
gling in full sight of land.[116]

At first glance, Serenus' long description appears to be an
accumulation of relatively unimportant details about his likes
and dislikes, descriptions of trifles such as his father's heavy
plates, how he likes his food, and so on. And it also seems to
be in great disorder, a mess of details. But behind this apparent disorder you can easily discern the real organization of the
text. There are three basic parts to the discourse. The first
part, the beginning of the quote, is devoted to Serenus' relation to wealth, possessions, his domestic and private life. The
second part—which begins "I resolve to obey the commands
of my teachers..."—this paragraph deals with Serenus' relation to public life and his political character. And in the third
part—which starts at "And in my literary studies..."—
Serenus speaks of his literary activity, the type of language he
prefers to employ, and so on. But we can also recognize here
the relation between death and immortality, or the question of
an enduring life in people's memories after death. So the three
themes treated in these paragraphs are (1) private or domestic
life; (2) public life; and (3) immortality or afterlife.

In the first part Serenus explains what he is willing to do,
and what he likes to do. He thereby also shows what he considers unimportant and to which he is indifferent. And all
these descriptions show Serenus' positive image and character.
He does not have great material needs in his domestic life, for
he is not attached to luxury. In the second paragraph he says
he is not enslaved by ambition. He does not want a great polit-

116. Seneca, "On the Tranquillity of Mind," I. 4–17.

ical career, but to be of service to others. And in the third paragraph he states that he is not seduced by high-flown rhetoric,
but prefers instead to adhere to useful speech. You can see that
in this way Serenus draws up a balance sheet of his choices, of
his freedom, and the result is not bad at all. Indeed, it is quite
positive. Serenus is attached to what is natural, to what is necessary, to what is useful (either for himself or his friends), and
is usually indifferent to the rest. Regarding these three fields
(private life, public life, and afterlife), well, all told, Serenus is
rather a good fellow. And his account also shows us the precise
topic of his examination, which is: what are the things that are
important to me, and what are the things to which I am indifferent? And he considers important things which really *are*
important.

But each of the three paragraphs is also divided into two
parts. After Serenus explains the importance or indifference
he attributes to things, there is a transitional moment when he
begins to make an objection to himself, when his mind begins
to waver. These transitional moments are marked by his use of
the word *animus*. Regarding the three topics already noted,
Serenus explains that despite the fact that he makes good
choices, that he disregards unimportant things, he nonetheless feels that his mind, his *animus*, is involuntarily moved.
And as a result, although he is not exactly inclined to behave
in an opposite fashion, he is still dazzled or aroused by the
things he previously thought unimportant. These involuntary
feelings are indications, he believes, that his *animus* is not
completely tranquil or stable, and this motivates his request
for a consultation. Serenus knows the theoretical principles
and practical rules of Stoicism, is usually able to put them into
operation, yet he still feels that these rules are not a permanent
matrix for his behavior, his feelings, and his thoughts.

Serenus' instability does not derive from his "sins," or from
the fact that he exists as a temporal being—as in Augustine,
for example. It stems from the fact that he has not yet succeeded in harmonizing his actions and thoughts with the ethical structure he has chosen for himself. It is as if Serenus were
a good pilot, he knows how to sail, there is no storm on the
horizon, yet he is stuck at sea and cannot reach the solid earth
because he does not possess the *tranquillitas,* the *firmitas,* which
comes from complete self-sovereignty. And Seneca's reply to
this self-examination and moral request is an exploration of
the nature of this stability of mind.

Self-testing

A third text, which also shows some of the differences in the
truth games involved in these self-examination exercises,
comes from the Discourses of Epictetus—where I think you
can find a third type of exercise quite different from the previous ones. There are numerous types of self-examination
techniques and practices in Epictetus, some of them resem-
bling both the evening examinations of Sextius and the general self-scrutiny of Serenus. But there is one form of examination which, I think, is very characteristic of Epictetus, and
which takes the form of a constant putting on trial of all our
representations. This technique is also related to the demand
for stability; for given the constant stream of representations
which flow into the mind, Epictetus' problem consists in
knowing how to distinguish those representations that he can
control from those that he cannot control, that incite involuntary emotions, feelings, behavior, etc., and that must therefore
be excluded from his mind. Epictetus' solution is that we must
adopt an attitude of permanent surveillance with regard to all
our representations, and he explains this attitude by employ-

ing two metaphors: the metaphor of the nightwatchman or
doorkeeper who does not admit anyone into his house or
palace without first checking his identity; and the metaphor of
the "money-changer"—what the Greeks called the ἀργυρο-
μαιβός—who, when a coin is very difficult to read, verifies the
authenticity of the currency, examines it, weighs it, verifies the
metal and effigy, and so on:

> The third topic has to do with cases of assent; it is con-
> cerned with the things that are plausible and attractive.
> For, just as Socrates used to tell us not to live a life unsub-
> jected to examination, so we ought not to accept a sense-
> impression unsubjected to examination, but should say,
> "Wait, allow me to see who you are and whence you
> come" (just as the night-watch say, "Show me your
> tokens"). "Do you have your tokens from nature, the ones
> which every sense-impression which is to be accepted
> must have?"[117]

These two metaphors are also found in early Christian
texts. Johannes Cassian [A.D. 360–435], for example, asked his
monks to scrutinize and test their own representations like
a doorkeeper or a money-changer.[118] In the case of Christian
self-examination, the monitoring of representations has the
specific intention of determining whether, under an apparently
innocent guise, the devil himself is not hiding. For in order
not to be trapped by what only seems to be innocent, in order
to avoid the devil's counterfeit coins, the Christian must deter-

---

117. Epictetus, *The Discourses as Reported by Arrian,* Trans. W. A. Oldfather,
III, 12.
118. Cf. Michel Foucault, "Sexuality and Solitude," 6.

mine where his thoughts and sense impressions come from, and what relation actually exists between a representation's apparent and real value. For Epictetus, however, the problem is not to determine the source of the impression (God or Satan) so as to judge whether it conceals something or not; his problem is rather to determine whether the impression represents something which depends upon him or not, i.e., whether it is accessible or not to his will. Its purpose is not to dispel the devil's illusions, but to guarantee self-mastery.

To foster mistrust of our representations, Epictetus proposes two kinds of exercises. One form is borrowed directly from the Sophists. And in this classical game of the sophistic schools, one of the students asked a question, and another student had to answer it without falling into the sophistic trap. An elementary example of this sophistic game is this one: Question: "Can a chariot go through a mouth?" Answer: "Yes. You yourself said the word *chariot*, and it went through your mouth." Epictetus criticized such exercises as unhelpful, and proposed another for the purpose of moral training. In this game there are also two partners. One of the partners states a fact, an event, and the other has to answer, as quickly as possible, whether this fact or event is good or evil, i.e., is within or beyond our control. We can see this exercise, for example, in the following text:

> As we exercise ourselves to meet the sophistical interrogations, so we ought also to exercise ourselves daily to meet the impression of our senses, because these too put interrogations to us. So-and-so's son is dead. Answer, "That lies outside the sphere of the moral purpose, it is not an evil." His father has disinherited So-and-so; what do you think of it? "That lies outside the sphere of the

moral purpose, it is not an evil." Caesar has condemned him. "That lies outside the sphere of the moral purpose, it is not an evil." He was grieved at all this. "That lies within the sphere of the moral purpose, it is an evil." He has borne up under it manfully. "That lies within the sphere of the moral purpose, it is a good." Now if we acquire this habit, we shall make progress; for we shall never give our assent to anything but that of which we get a convincing sense-impression.[119]

There is another exercise Epictetus describes which has the same object, but the form is closer to those employed later in the Christian tradition. It consists in walking through the streets of the city and asking yourself whether any representation that happens to come to your mind depends upon your will or not. If it does not lie within the province of moral purpose and will, then it must be rejected:

Go out of the house at early dawn, and no matter whom you see or whom you hear, examine him and then answer as you would to a question. What did you see? A handsome man or a handsome woman? Apply your rule. Is it outside the province of the moral purpose, or inside? Outside. Away with it. What did you see? A man in grief over the death of his child? Apply your rule. Death lies outside the province of the moral purpose. Out of the way with it. Did a Consul meet you? Apply your rule. What sort of thing is a consulship? Outside the province of the moral purpose, or inside? Outside. Away with it, too, it

119. Epictetus, *The Discourses as Reported by Arrian,* III, 8.

does not meet the test; throw it away, it does not concern you. If we had kept doing this and had exercised ourselves from dawn till dark with this principle in mind—by the gods, something would have been achieved![120]

As you can see, Epictetus wants us to constitute a world of representations where nothing can intrude which is not subject to the sovereignty of our will. So, again, self-sovereignty is the organizing principle of this form of self-examination.

I would have liked to have analyzed two more texts from Marcus Aurelius, but given the hour, I have no time left for this. So I would now like to turn to my conclusions.

In reading these texts about self-examination and underlining the differences between them, I wanted to show you, first, that there is a noticeable shift in the parrhesiastic practices between the "master" and the "disciple." Previously, when *parrhesia* appeared in the context of spiritual guidance, the master was the one who disclosed the truth about the disciple. In these exercises, the master still uses frankness of speech with the disciple in order to help him become aware of the faults he cannot see (Seneca uses *parrhesia* towards Serenus, Epictetus uses *parrhesia* towards his disciples); but now the use of *parrhesia* is put increasingly upon the disciple as his own duty towards himself. At this point the truth about the disciple is not disclosed solely through the parrhesiastic discourse of the master, or only in the dialogue between the master and the disciple or interlocutor. The truth about the disciple emerges from a personal relation which he establish-

---

120. *Ibid.*, 3. Cf. Michel Foucault, *Le Souci de soi*, 79–81; Foucault interview: "On the Genealogy of Ethics," 249.

es with himself: and this truth can now be disclosed either to himself (as in the first example from Seneca) or to someone else (as in the second example from Seneca). And the disciple must also test himself, and check to see whether he is able to achieve self-mastery (as in the examples from Epictetus).

Secondly, it is not sufficient to analyze this personal relation of self-understanding as merely deriving from the general principle *"gnothi seauton"*—"know thyself." Of course, in a certain general sense it can be derived from this principle, but we cannot stop at this point. For the various relationships which one has to oneself are embedded in very precise techniques which take the form of spiritual exercises—some of them dealing with deeds, others with states of equilibrium of the soul, others with the flow of representations, and so on.

Third point. In all these different exercises, what is at stake is not the disclosure of a secret which has to excavated from out of the depths of the soul. What is at stake is the *relation* of the self to truth or to some rational principles. Recall that the question which motivated Seneca's evening self-examination was: Did I bring into play those principles of behavior I know very well, but, as it sometimes happens, I do not always conform to or always apply? Another question was: Am I able to adhere to the principles I am familiar with, I agree with, and which I practice most of the time? For that was Serenus' question. Or the question Epictetus raised in the exercises I was just discussing: Am I able to react to any kind of representation which shows itself to me in conformity with my adopted rational rules? What we have to underline here is this: if the truth of the self in these exercises is nothing other than the *relation* of the self to truth, then this truth is not purely theoretical. The truth of the self involves, on the one hand, a set of rational principles which are grounded in general statements about the world, human life, necessity, happiness, freedom, and so on, and, on the other hand, practical rules for behavior. And the question which is raised in these different exercises is oriented towards the following problem: Are we familiar enough with these rational principles? Are they sufficiently well-established in our minds to become practical rules for our everyday behavior? And the problem of memory is at the heart of these techniques, but in the form of an attempt to remind ourselves of what we have done, thought, or felt so that we may reactivate our rational principles, thus making them as permanent and as effective as possible in our life. These exercises are part of what we could call an "aesthetics of the self." For one does not have to take up a position or role towards oneself as that of a judge pronouncing a verdict. One can comport oneself towards oneself in the role of a technician, of a craftsman, of an artist, who from time to time stops working, examines what he is doing, reminds himself of the rules of his art, and compares these rules with what he has achieved thus far. This metaphor of the artist who stops working, steps back, gains a distant perspective, and examines what he is actually doing with the principles of his art can be found in Plutarch's essay, "On the Control of Anger" [Περὶ ἀοργησίας].[121]

---

121. Plutarch writes: "A good plan, as it seems to me...is that which painters follow: they scrutinize their productions from time to time before they finish them. They do this because, by withdrawing their gaze and by inspecting their work often, they are able to form a fresh judgment, and one which is more likely to seize upon any slight discrepancy, such as the familiarity of uninterrupted contemplation will conceal." ["On the Control of Anger," Trans. W. C. Helmbold, 452f–453a]

Concluding Remarks

And now a few words about this seminar.

The point of departure. My intention was not to deal with the problem of truth, but with the problem of the truth-teller, or of truth-telling as an activity. By this I mean that, for me, it was not a question of analyzing the internal or external criteria that would enable the Greeks and Romans, or anyone else, to recognize whether a statement or proposition is true or not. At issue for me was rather the attempt to consider truth-telling as a specific activity, or as a role. But even in the framework of this general question of the role of the truth-teller in a society, there were several possible ways to conduct the analysis. For instance, I could have compared the role and status of truth-tellers in Greek society, Christian societies, non-Christian societies—the role of the prophet as a truth-teller, the role of the oracle as a truth-teller, the role of the poet, of the expert, of the preacher, and so on. But, in fact, my intention was not to conduct a sociological description of the different possible roles for truth-tellers in different societies. What I wanted to analyze was how the truth-teller's role was variously problematized in Greek philosophy. And what I wanted to show you was that if Greek philosophy has raised the problem of truth from the point of view of the criteria for true statements and sound reasoning, this same Greek philosophy has also raised the question of truth from the point of view of truth-telling as an activity. It has raised questions like: Who is able to tell the truth? What are the moral, the ethical, and the spiritual conditions which entitle someone to present himself as, and to be considered as, a truth-teller? About what topics is it important to tell the truth? (About the world? About nature? About the city? About behavior? About man?) What are the consequences of telling the truth? What are its anticipated positive effects for the city, for the city's rulers, for the individual?, etc. And finally: What is the relation between the activity of truth-telling and the exercise of power? Should truth-telling be brought into coincidence with the exercise of power, or should these activities be completely independent and kept separate? Are they separable, or do they require one another? These four questions about truth-telling as an activity—who is able to tell the truth, about what, with what consequences, and with what relation to power—seem to have emerged as philosophical problems towards the end of the Fifth Century around Socrates, especially through his confrontations with the Sophists about politics, rhetorics, and ethics.

And I would say that the problematization of truth which characterizes both the end of Presocratic philosophy and the beginning of the kind of philosophy which is still ours today, this problematization of truth has two sides, two major aspects. One side is concerned with ensuring that the process of reasoning is correct in determining whether a statement is true (or concerns itself with our ability to gain access to the truth). And the other side is concerned with the question: What is the importance for the individual and for the society of telling the truth, of knowing the truth, of having people who tell the truth, as well as knowing how to recognize them? With that side which is concerned with determining how to ensure that a statement is true we have the roots of the great tradition in Western philosophy which I would like to call the "analytics of truth." And on the other side, concerned with the question of the importance of telling the truth, knowing who is able to tell the truth, and knowing why we should tell the truth, we have the roots of what we could call the "critical" tradition in the West. And here you will recognize one of my targets in this seminar, namely, to construct a genealogy of the critical attitude in Western philosophy. That constituted the general objective target of this seminar.

From the methodological point of view, I would like to underscore the following theme. As you may have noticed, I utilized the word *problematization* frequently in this seminar without providing you with an explanation of its meaning. I told you very briefly that what I intended to analyze in most of my work was neither past people's behavior (which is something that belongs to the field of social history), nor ideas in their representative values. What I tried to do from the beginning was to analyze the process of "problematization"— which means: how and why certain things (behavior, phenomena, processes) became a *problem*.[122] Why, for example, certain forms of behavior were characterized and classified as "madness" while other similar forms were completely neglected at a given historical moment; the same thing for crime and delinquency, the same question of problematization for sexuality.

Some people have interpreted this type of analysis as a form of "historical idealism," but I think that such an analysis is completely different. For when I say that I am studying the "problematization" of madness, crime, or sexuality, it is not a way of denying the reality of such phenomena. On the contrary, I have tried to show that it was precisely some real existent in the world which was the target of social regulation at a given moment. The question I raise is this one: How and why were very different things in the world gathered together, characterized, analyzed, and treated as, for example, "mental illness"? What are the elements which are relevant for a given "problematization"? And even if I won't say that what is char-

---

122. Cf. Michel Foucault, *L'Usage des plaisirs,* 16–19.

acterized as "schizophrenia" corresponds to something real in the world, this has nothing to do with idealism. For I think there is a relation between the thing which is problematized and the process of problematization. The problematization is an "answer" to a concrete situation which is real.

There is also a mistaken interpretation according to which my analysis of a given problematization is without any historical context, as if it were a spontaneous process coming from anywhere. In fact, however, I have tried to show, for instance, that the new problematization of illness or physical disease at the end of the 18th Century was very directly linked to a modification in various practices, or to the development of a new social reaction to diseases, or to the challenge posed by certain processes, and so on. But we have to understand very clearly, I think, that a given problematization is not an effect or consequence of a historical context or situation, but is an answer given by definite individuals (although you may find this same answer given in a series of texts, and at a certain point the answer may become so general that it also becomes anonymous).

For example, with regard to the way that *parrhesia* was problematized at a given moment, we can see that there are specific Socratic-Platonic answers to the questions: How can we recognize someone as a *parrhesiastes*? What is the importance of having a *parrhesiastes* for the city? What is the training of a good *parrhesiastes*?—answers which were given by Socrates or Plato. These answers are not collective ones from any sort of collective unconscious. And the fact that an answer is neither a representation nor an effect of a situation does not mean that it answers to nothing, that it is a pure dream, or an "anti-creation." A problematization is always a kind of creation; but a creation in the sense that, given a certain situation, you cannot infer that this kind of problematization will follow. Given a certain problematization, you can only understand why this kind of answer appears as a reply to some concrete and specific aspect of the world. There is the relation of thought and reality in the process of problematization. And that is the reason why I think that it is possible to give an analysis of a specific problematization as the history of an answer—the original, specific, and singular answer of thought—to a certain situation. And it is this kind of specific relation between truth and reality which I have tried to analyze in the various problematizations of *parrhesia*.

Bibliography

STUDIES ON *PARRHESIA*

Ancient Authors

PHILODEMUS. Περὶ παρρησίας. Ed. Alexander Olivleri; Leipzig: B. G. Teubneri, 1914.

PLUTARCH. "How to Tell a Flatterer from a Friend," Trans. Frank Cole Babbitt in *Plutarch's Moralia*, Vol. 1; Cambridge and London: Harvard & Heinemann, 1969 (Loeb Classical Library); 263–395.

Modern Authors

BARTELINK, Gerhardus Johannes Marinus. "Quelques observations sur παρρησία dans la littérature paléo-chrétienne," in *Graecitas et Latinitas Christianorum primaeva*, Supp. III; Nijmegen: Dekker & Van de Vegt, 1970; 5–57.

COQUIN, R. G. "Le thème de la παρρησία et ses expressions symboliques dans les rites d'initiation à Antioche," in *Proche-Orient chrétien* 20 (1970): 3–19.

DEWITT, Norman W. "Parrhesiastic Poems of Horace," *Classical Philology* 30 (1935): 312–319.

ENGELS, L. "Fiducia dans la Vulgate, Le problème de la traduction παρρησία-fiducia," in *Graecitas et Latinitas Christianorum primaeva*, Supp. I; Nijmegen: Dekker & Van de Vegt, 1964; 97–141.

GIGANTE, Marcello. "Filodemo sulla libertà di parola," in his *Ricerche Filodemee;* Napoli: Gaetano Macchiaroli Editore, 1969; 41–61.

—. "Philodème: Sur la liberté de parole." in *Actes du VIIIᵉ Congrés (Paris, 5–10 avril 1968)*, Association Guillaume Budé; Paris: Société d'Édition "Les Belles Lettres," 1969; 196–217 [French translation of above].

—. "Motivi paideutici nell' opera filodemea sulla libertà di parola." *Cronache Ercolanesi* 4 (1974): 38–39.

HOLSTEIN, H. "La παρρησία dans le Nouveau Testament," in *Bible et vie chrétienne* 53 (1963): 45–54.

JAEGER, Hasso. "Παρρησία et fiducia. Étude spirituelle des mots," in *Studia Patristica* 1 (Berlin, 1957): 221–239.

JOÜON, Paul. "Divers sens de παρρησία dans le Nouveau Testament," *Recherches de Science religieuse* 30 (1940): 239–242.

LAMPE, C.W.H. "Παρρησία" in *A Patristic Greek Lexicon;* Oxford, 1968; cols. 1044–1046 .

LIDDELL, Henry G. & SCOTT, Robert. "Παρρησία" in *A Greek-English Lexicon* Oxford: Clarendon Press, 1968 [Ninth Edition]; 1344.

MIQUEL, Pierre. "Παρρησία" in *Dictionnaire de Spiritualité*, Vol. 12; Paris: Beauchesne, 1984; cols. 260–267.

MOMIGLIANO, Arnaldo. "Freedom of Speech in Antiquity" in Philip P. Wiener, ed. *Dictionary of the History of Ideas*, Vol. 2; New York: Charles Scribner's Sons, 1973; 252–263.

PETERSON, Erik. "Zur Bedeutungsgeschichte von Παρρησία," in Wilhelm Koepp, ed., *Reinhold Seeberg Festschrift*, Vol. 1: Zur Theorie des Christentums; Leipzig: A. Deichertsche Verlagsbuchhandlung D. Werner Scholl, 1929; 283–297.

PHILIPPSON, Robert. Rezension von Philodemi, Περὶ παρρησίας; *Berliner Philologische Wochenschrift* 36 (1916): 677–688.

RADIN, Max. "Freedom of Speech in Ancient Athens," *American Journal of Philology* 48 (1927): 215–230.

RAHNER, Karl. "Παρρησία von der Apostolatstugend des Christen," *Geist und Leben* 31 (1958): 1–6.

RODRIGUEZ, J. V. "Παρρησία teresiana," *Revista de Espiritualidad* 40 (1981): 527–573.

SCARPAT, Giuseppe. *Parrhesia. Storia del termine e delle sue traduzioni in Latino*; Brescia: Paideia Editrice, 1964.

SCHLIER, Heinrich. "Παρρησία, παρρησιάζομαι" in Gerhard Kittel, ed., *Theological Dictionary of the New Testament*, Vol. 5; Grand Rapids: Wm. B. Eerdmans, 1967; 871–886.

SMOLDERS, D. "L'audace de l'apôtre selon saint Paul, Le thème de la παρρησία," *Collectanea Mechliniensia* 43 (Louvain, 1958): 1–30; 117–133.

STÄHLIN, Wilhelm. "Parousia und Parrhesia," in Leo Scheffczyk, Werner Deffloff, und Richard Heinzmann, eds., *Wahrheit und Verkündigung*; Paderborn: Schoningh, 1967; 229–235.

STEIDLE, B. "Παρρησία-praesumptio in der Klosterregel St. Benedikts," in *Zeugnis des Geistes;* Beuron: Beuroner Kunstverlag, 1947; 44–61.

TOMADAKES, N. B. Παρρησία-παρρησιαστικός" in *Epèteris Hetaireias Byzantinôn Spoudôn* 33 (1964): fasc. 1.

VAN UNNIK, W. C. *De Semitische Achtergrond van* Παρρησία *In Het Nieuwe Testament*; Amsterdam: Noord-Hollandsche Uitg. Mij., 1962.

—. "The Christian's Freedom of Speech in the New Testament," *Bulletin of the John Rylands Library* 44 (1962): 466–488.

—. "Παρρησία in the 'Catechetical Homilies' of Theodore of Mopsuestia," in *Mélanges offerts à Mademoiselle Christine Mohrmann*; Utrecht-Anvers, 1963; 12–22.

VOSTER, W. S., "The Meaning of Παρρησία in the Epistle to the Hebrews," *Neotestamentica* 5 (1971): 51–59.

Ancient Authors Cited

ARISTOTLE. *Constitution of Athens*, Trans. F. G. Kenyon in *The Complete Works of Aristotle*. Ed. J. Barnes; Princeton: Princeton U. Press, 1984, Vol. 2.

—. *Nicomachean Ethics*, Trans. W. D. Ross, revised by J. O. Urmson in *The Complete Works of Aristotle, op. cit.*, Vol. 2.

DEMOSTHENES. "Third Philippic," Trans. J. H. Vince in *Demosthenes I: Olynthiacs, Philippics and Minor Orations*; Cambridge and London: Harvard & Heinemann, 1930 (Loeb Classical Library).

DIO CHRYSOSTOM. "The Fourth Discourse on Kingship," "The Fifth Discourse: A Libyan Myth," and "The Ninth, or Isthmian, Discourse" in *Dio Chrysostom,* Vol. 1; Trans. J. W . Cohoon; Cambridge and London: Harvard & Heinemann, 1971 (Loeb Classical Library).

DIOGENES LAERTIUS. *Lives of Eminent Philosophers.* Trans. R. D. Hicks; 2 Vols.; Cambridge and London: Harvard & Heinemann, 1980 (Loeb Classical Library).

EPICTETUS. *The Discourses as Reported by Arrian.* Trans. W. A. Oldfather; 2 Vols.; Cambridge and London: Harvard & Heinemann, 1926–1928 (Loeb Classical Library).

EURIPIDES. *The Bacchae; Ion; The Women of Troy;* in *The Bacchae and Other Plays.* Trans. Philip Vellacott; New York: Penguin Books, 1980.

—. *Electra* in *Medea and Other Plays,* Trans. Philip Vellacott; New York: Penguin Books, 1982.

—. *Hippolytus,* in *Three Plays.* Trans. Philip Vellacott; New York: Penguin Books, 1979.

—. *The Suppliant Women; The Phoenician Women; Orestes* in *Orestes and Other Plays.* Trans. Philip Vellacott; New York: Penguin Books, 1983.

—. *Ion.* Trans. Ronald Frederick Willetts in *Euripides III;* Chicago: U. of Chicago Press, 1974.

GALEN. "The Diagnosis and Cure of the Soul's Passions" in *On the Passions and Errors of the Soul.* Trans. Paul W. Harkin; Ohio State U. Press, 1963; 25–69.

ISOCRATES. "To Nicocles." Trans. George Norlin in *Isocrates,* Vol. 1; Cambridge and London: Harvard & Heinemann, 1968 (Loeb Classical Library).

—. "Areopagitus," "On the Peace." Trans. George Norlin in *Isocrates,*

Vol. 2; Cambridge and London: Harvard & Heinemann, 1968.

JULIAN. "To the Uneducated Cynics." Trans. Wilmer Cave Wright in *The Works of Emperor Julian*, Vol. 2; London and New York: Heinemann & The Macmillan Co., 1913 (Loeb Classical Library).

LUCIAN. "The Dead Come to Life, or The Fisherman." Trans. A. M. Harman in *The Works of Lucian*, Vol. 3; Cambridge and London: Harvard & Heinemann, 1962 (Loeb Classical Library).

—. "The Passing of Peregrinus," "The Runaways." Trans. A. M. Harman in *The Works of Lucian*, Vol. 5; op. *cit.*

MUSONIUS RUFUS. "On Training," in Cora E. Lutz, *Musonius Rufus*; New Haven: Yale U. Press, 1947; 53–57.

PLATO. *Gorgias*. Trans. R. E. Allen in his *The Dialogues of Plato*, Vol. 1; New Haven: Yale U. Press, 1984.

—. *Laches*. Trans. W. R. M. Lamb in *Plato: Laches, Protagoras, Meno, Euthydemus;* Cambridge and London: Harvard & Heinemann, 1977 (Loeb Classical Library).

—. *Republic,* Trans. F. M. Cornford; London: Oxford U. Press, 1963.

—. *The Laws.* Trans. Thomas L. Pangle; New York: Basic Books, 1980.

—. *Letter VII.* Trans. L. A. Post in Edith Hamilton & Hunington Cairnes, eds., *Plato. The Collected Dialogues*; New York: Random House, 1966.

PLUTARCH. "The Education of Children." Trans. Frank Cole Babbitt in *Plutarch's Moralia*, Vol. 1; Cambridge and London: Harvard & Heinemann, 1969 (Loeb Classical Library).

—. "On the Control of Anger," "Concerning Talkativeness." Trans. W. C. Helmbold in *Plutarch's Moralia*, Vol. 6; Cambridge and London: Harvard & Heinemann, 1962 (Loeb Classical Library).

—. "Stoic Self-Contradictions." Trans. Harold Cherniss in *Plutarch's Moralia*, Vol. 13, part 2; Cambridge and London: Harvard & Heinemann, 1976 (Loeb Classical Library).

QUINTILLIAN. *The Institutio Oratoria of Quintillian.* Trans. H. E. Butler; London & New York: Heinemann & G. P. Putnam's Sons, 1921–1933 (Loeb Classical Library).

SENECA. "On Anger," "On Tranquillity of Mind." Trans. John W. Basore in *Moral Essays*, 3 vols.; Cambridge & London: Harvard & Heinemann, 1928 (Loeb Classical Library).

THEOGNIS. *Elegies.* Trans. Dorothea Wender in *Hesiod and Theognis;* New York: Penguin Books, 1982.

XENOPHON. *Oeconomicus.* Trans. Carnes Lordin in Leo Strauss's *Xenophon's Socratic Discourses;* Ithaca: Cornell U. Press, 1970; 1–80.

PSEUDO-XENOPHON [The Old Oligarch]. *The Constitution of the Athenians.* Trans. Hartvig Frisch in his *The Constitution of the Athenians: A Philological-Historical Analysis of pseudo-Xenophon's Treatise De Re Publica Atheniensium;* Copenhagen: Glydedalske Boghandel-Nordisk Forlag, 1942.

MODERN AUTHORS CITED

BONNER, Robert J. *Aspects of Athenian Democracy.* Berkeley: U. of California Press, 1933 [Chapter IV: Freedom of Speech].

DEWITT, Norman W. "Organization and Procedure in Epicurean Groups." *Classical Philology* 31 (1936): 205–211.

—. "Epicurean *Contubernium*," *Transactions and Proceedings of the American Philological Association* 67 (1936): 55–63.

—. *Epicurus and His Philosophy.* Minneapolis: U. of Minnesota Press, 1954 [Chapter V: The New School in Athens].

DIELS, Hermann. *Die Fragmente der Vorsokratiker.* Ed. W. Kranz; Berlin, 1951.

DOVER, K. J. "Classical Greek Attitudes to Sexual Behavior." *Arethusa* 6 (1973): 59–73.

FOUCAULT, Michel. "Sexuality and Solitude" [with Richard Sennett]. *London Review of Books,* 21 May–3 June 1982; 3–7.

—. "On the Genealogy of Ethics: An Overview of Work in Progress." Interview with Hubert L. Dreyfus and Paul Rabinow in their *Michel Foucault: Beyond Structuralism and Hermeneutics* [Second Edition]; Chicago: U. of Chicago Press, 1983; 229–252. An abridged version of this interview appeared in *Vanity Fair* (Vol. 46, November 1983): 61–69.

—. *The Use of Pleasure.* New York: Random House, 1995.

—. *The Care of the Self.* New York: Random House, 1986.

GIGANTE, Marcello. "'Philosophia Medicans' in Filodemo," *Cronache Ercolanesi* 5 (1975): 53–61.

HADOT, Pierre. *Exercises spirituels et philosophie antique.* Paris: Études augustiennes, 1981.

HIJMANS, Benjamin L. *Askesis: Notes on Epictetus' Educational System.* (Wijsgerige teksten en studies, 2) Assem, Van Gorcum, 1959.

JAEGER, Werner. *Paideia: The Ideals of Greek Culture.* Trans. Gilbert Highet; New York: Oxford U. Press, 1945.

JONES, A.H.M. "The Athenian Democracy and its Critics," in his *Athenian Democracy.* Oxford: Basil Blackwell, 1957; 41–72.

JONES, Christopher P. *The Roman World of Dio Chrysostom.* Cambridge: Harvard U. Press, 1978.

LUTZ, Cora E. *Musonius Rufus.* New Haven: Yale U. Press, 1942.

OWEN, A.S. *Euripides, Ion.* Oxford: Clarendon Press, 1957.

SAYRE, Ferrand. *Diogenes of Sinope: A Study of Greek Cynicism.* Baltimore: J.H. Furst Co., 1938.

VANDENBROUCKE, François. "Démon," *Dictionnaire de Spiritualité,* Vol. 3, 1957; cols. 141–238.

Semiotext(e) Native Agents

Airless Spaces
Shulamith Firestone

Aliens & Anorexia
Chris Kraus

If You're a Girl
Ann Rower

Indivisible
Fanny Howe

Hannibal Lecter, My Father
Kathy Acker

I Love Dick
Chris Kraus

How I Became One of the Invisible
David Rattray

Leash
Jane DeLynn

Not Me
Eileen Myles

**The Passionate Mistakes and Intricate Corruptions
of One Girl in America**
Michelle Tea

Semiotext(e) Foreign Agents

Assassination Rhapsody
Derek Pell

Behold Metatron, the Recording Angel
Sol Yurick

Bolo'Bolo
P.M.

Chaosophy
Félix Guattari

Civilization and Its Rebellion
Julia Kristeva

Crepuscular Dawn: The Genetic Bomb
Paul Virilio & Sylvère Lotringer

Cruel Little Wars
Alain Joxe

Driftworks
Jean-François Lyotard

Ecstacy of Communication
Jean Baudrillard

Fearless Speech
Michel Foucault

Semiotext(e) Double Agents

Archeology of Violence
Pierre Clastres

Fatal Strategies
Jean Baudrillard

Foucault Live: The Collected Interviews of Michel Foucault
Sylvère Lotringer, ed.

Hatred of Capitalism: A Reader
Chris Kraus & Sylvère Lotringer, eds.

Imported
Rainer Ganhal, ed.

The Aesthetics of Disappearance
Paul Virilio

The Collected Interviews of William S. Burroughs
Sylvère Lotringer, ed.